Dogs Don't Cook

and what we can learn from them

Regine Kohler ND

Copyright © 2020

All rights reserved. This book or any portion thereof may not be reproduced or used in any manner whatsoever without the express written permission of the author except for the use of brief quotations in a book review.

Printed in Australia. First Printing 2020

ISBN: 978-0-6489666-0-9

White Light Publishing

whitelightuniversal.com.au

*Gratitude to all that have taught me,
the animals, plants and some wise humans.*

*Special thanks to Lotti and all the other animals who
shared their life with me, may we catch up again sometime.*

Preface

When all else fails,
And the ship lost all its sails
hug the dog and listen to the plants
all you need to know is in their chants

I have written this book to remind my fellow human travellers of what is inherently known to all of us. If we deeply look into ourselves, we all know what is best for this earth, all living beings and indeed, ourselves. We have forgotten we are made from and by nature, we have become arrogant and don't take much interest how we mess up our own 'nest' and that of other beings who mind their own business, they just want to live their lives and be happy like us.

So why don't we act on it and behave like a responsible part of this earthly community? This question I have asked myself many times and so far, I cannot find an answer apart from greed and power by those that hold authority and the many people that follow them. Nevertheless, when it comes to basics, I believe most people want to be happy, safe, have enough to eat, and enjoy good friends without harming anyone else. Despite what is happening on the planet I am not discouraged to give up learning and sharing, so others may remember to re-connect with the world around us, which was known intimately to our ancestors. How else would they have had the knowledge about the healing effect of thousands of plants and survive millions of years unless they lived in unison with them?

I am aware of the fact that I am only a tiny speck in the greatness of the cosmos, at the same time I can influence my surroundings with my thoughts and actions. Along the way of learning I also get to know myself better, find out what makes me tick and what ruffles my feathers, it is also my own journey.

My aim is to unravel some misunderstandings, explain in simple terms the interplay between the outside and the inside world of us as humans and show that the natural world of which we are a part of, as our pets are, has the same rules and laws for all beings on earth. Caring for and living with other beings, in our case our closest companions, the dogs and cats, (and certainly any other small and large animal), does not need to have misunderstandings and problems when we observe nature's guidelines. Being receptive we can learn from our furry teachers as well; they readily share their natural wisdom with anyone who wants to listen.

Copernicus, Galileo and Kepler shifted the world view from a geocentric idea, the earth was thought to be in the centre of the universe until then; to a heliocentric one, where the planets revolve around the sun. Descartes and Newton in the 17th century began to formulate a new concept of nature as an impersonal and inert machine and physical reality was nothing more than particles in motion and everything resulted from their mechanical motion. This idea was transferred to the human body, also viewed as a machine. This certainly is only a crude description of their work, without a question they contributed hugely to physics, chemistry, engineering, mathematics, they are termed the fathers of modern science.

Their work gave rise to the thought that science could unravel all of nature and we would possess the truth about the universe and everything else in it. The age of reason, the industrial age, the nuclear age, the space age and the information age followed. I feel we still have to deal with a strong residue of the mechanistic viewpoint regarding the way we treat our environment, the disregard of nature with its diverse inhabitants and especially concerning the treatment of animals, deemed below humans.

We certainly made huge steps in physics, astronomy, medicine and engineering, explaining many natural phenomena and invent technologies, which to our ancestors would fall under the term of mysticism. Science can in many cases explain a metaphysical phenomenon, nevertheless there is much to be discovered.

Many ancient books and manuscripts written on animal skin, copper, papyrus, clay tablets, stones and inscriptions of different kinds have been inherited and discovered from our distant ancestors which have enlightened us how the ancient people saw the world and its wonders. To be fair to the ancients, they knew about astronomical occurrences, the cosmos, even had knowledge about certain stars we only discovered some years ago. Cultures like the Mayas, Incas, Indians, the Indian nations on the American continent, the Egyptians and many more around the world knew about the earth history, flora and fauna, the cosmic calendar, much of which was passed on from generation to generation.

More recently great minds brought us further in understanding physics, the cosmos and our place in it, best known to everyone are Albert Einstein, Nikola Tesla, Heisenberg and Bohr and many other contemporary scientists. We have been fortunate to have wise men and women enlightening us about ourselves as conscious beings sitting in the great classroom of the earth, in the school we call universe. Especially in the last 120 years science and technology has changed our world to that extend that many of us have a problem to follow. Just one example from my own training concerning the view of an atom. In technical college I learned that atoms consist of a nucleus, a centre, and electrons circling this centre at various distances, looking like a little solar system. Today we know that the atom looks like a wave of energy rather than particles of things.

It seems to me that the more we research something, more puzzle pieces are found and the need for more exploration is ever present. Do we really need to be able to explain everything to the detail? Does it make our lives better or happier? Doesn't it take away the wonderment, the fascination, the feeling that there is something greater out there, to evoke a humble feeling to honour and be thankful for the world we live in?

The quest for knowledge is often seen as a noble enterprise, to strive for at any price. We think it makes us superior to all others and as a consequence we are allowed to use and abuse everything in the name of science. I believe our first lesson on this planet is to get to know ourselves and how we fit into the 'spider web' of organisms on earth. We are all wired to the collective. I also believe we can learn from nature in this regard, especially from animals and we are very fortunate when we have a four-legged friend as a faithful companion and valuable teacher.

I am a holistic medicine practitioner, not a medical doctor or a vet and do not claim to fix or heal anyone. I do not want to talk 'science' in ways that aren't easy to understand and/or to put in practice, and certainly don't want to use technical jargon to impress anyone. I have a 'down to earth' and 'common sense' approach and use the 'kiss' rule: keep it simple stupid, so everyone can follow and practice my suggestions if it rings a bell for them.

To make it easier for everyone to understand, I researched and detailed only certain differences between humans and their pets, concerning the physical, physiological and psychological make up I thought were important for understanding another species and what could possibly contribute to the wellbeing of both. After all pets and humans live under one roof, sharing life. Furthermore, I offer ideas and tricks to improve and make life easier and healthier, so the time spent together with our furry companions is a happy one.

I do not have solutions for everything, just writing about my experiences and insights as another 'inmate' of this planet who cares about everything around me. I sincerely hope to speak to you as an entertaining and engaging researcher presenting sensible ideas to enhance life for both, people and pets. If, what I am writing rings true and makes sense, please share with others. Health and wellbeing are really easy, just look into nature, learn from the animals, observe and talk your pet and listen to the answers, take notice of the plants. We are here to learn.

This book is written as a guide to a better life together with our animals, not to diagnose or to replace any veterinary or medical treatments.

Introduction

My older 'sister' Peggy who brought me up

My best playmate in early childhood, a Collie named Peggy, who guarded me day and night, and must have had a 'paw' in shaping my life for the future.

As a child I always had a sense of wonder about nature and its 'inhabitants'. From an early age I spent much time sitting in the garden and observing beetles, ants and other bugs busily moving about and imagining being in their world. Occasionally I imprisoned them in matchboxes to study and watch them further, most probably to the consternation of those bugs. Our family lived on a large block on the banks of a river which they bought with help of the grandparents and build our house in 1948. In those days it was important to have a garden, even people living in city apartments grew fruit and vegetables in garden plots in designated areas outside the city, nearest to where they lived.

My father designed and planted the garden over the many years. We had vegetables from summer into winter, many different vegetable, fruit trees and delicious strawberries. Growing cacti was his hobby and occasionally a photo of a specific flowering plant he had grown appeared in the newspaper. He provided a small part of our garden for me to plant and look after when I was about 3 or 4 years old. Growing up in Germany one had to make the most of summertime, which was spent outdoors from morning until nightfall, often barefoot. My parents put me in leather pants, the traditional 'Lederhosen' so I wouldn't wreck too many clothes.

Father's tireless work in the garden and being close to the earth and plants, surely must have had some influence on me concerning nature. My mother's practical ways of running the household and her D.I.Y. attitude as well as going to work, also made a mark on me, probably paved the way to my common-sense attitude throughout my life. Much later, when our house was pulled down to make way for a bridge, I also learned about the impermanence of everything, including us humans.

Those early years clearly imprinted me with natures wisdom, as a small child is more intuitive and open and subconsciously picks up information of its surroundings. I remember I always had the wish to talk to animals and plants, not in a superior manner as I realized many years ago, but as an equal, as another vibration in a vibrational environment, in a vibrational cosmos. Even in my early childhood I felt other children were cruel to each other. Another incident which I remember clearly, involved a horse pulling a cart whose owner whipped it right in front of my mother and me standing on the footpath which touched me deeply. I could never understand why people hurt animals who cannot defend themselves and even thinking about it upsets me.

One of my strengths, as mentioned earlier, is to look at everything with a common-sense attitude, helping me to navigate through obstacles and always find a practical solution, even for little problems. Chapter 6 is explaining about common sense and how this is really inherent in everyone.

There weren't many years in my life I spent without animals or a garden. Horses, goats, chicken, geese, ducks, birds and cats came and went, but the dogs always stayed with me. I am eternally grateful to all of those animals (not to forget the plants) for teaching me so much about life and myself. They still do.

It is my offering to everyone, sharing the wisdom and insight I acquired in my life and ask the animal spirits to look kindly on us, I humbly acknowledge there is so much to learn. Because of this connection with nature, it was just 'natural' to study holistic medicine later in life and make it my profession. These formal studies, as well as the informal studies and my in depth training at the University of Life, confirmed the fact of our connectedness and deepened my beliefs that our lives, may that be humans, animals or plants, are intertwined and totally dependent on each other, nature, our planet and the laws of the universe. Indeed, it is now a fact in physics that there is no 'dead' matter, all is just frequency, a vibration.

We are all children of Mother Nature in the great cycle of life, we are all made out of similar stuff based on atoms, molecules and electromagnetic fields of information. One day our 'spacesuits', our bodies, will be recycled back into her arms again when we die and fertilize the earth with our, hopefully not too toxic bodies. Anything that de-composes (take note of the word.) is separated into its building blocks and re-used again. Nature eventually composes other organisms from it, including another human. So, in reality we are composed from all kinds of organisms that came before us. The energy contained in our bodies, and in any other organism, that drives the 'motor' of our being, must go somewhere else or be changed into another form. We will find out one day.

Over time my naturopathic treatments and consultations didn't stop with humans I eventually included pets and advised their carers on the best diet for the animals and simple home treatments. My laser therapy, acupuncture without needles, not only helped many human clients but also some dogs with injuries caused by falling out of trucks, arthritic complaints or back issues.

Originally my aim was to write a book about pet health, explaining and putting emphasis on their need for a species correct nutrition and other topics for keeping them healthy and happy. I could see pets had become a commodity, a cash cow (sorry cows.) for big companies inventing all kinds of so-called pet foods and other articles they don't need.

Some years ago, I translated manuals and a website for a holistic vet from German into English, learning so much from his writings and treatments. He also established, probably close to 20 years ago, a business selling dried kibble, dried under 40° C to retain the goodness of the ingredients. The only company that takes care of their product, as far as I know in the Western World.

Soon I felt that I had to digress further, showing that the path we have taken not only concerns the animals in our care, but also ourselves and indeed the whole planet; the possibility to recognize ourselves, who we really are through our four-legged companions and eventually walk towards better health together. This could be a strong possibility for everyone. No one is separate from all others; dogs and cats live within families, share the space and daily routine. Wisdom about a good life is easily gained not only by learning from others, but also observing our pets and nature around us.

It really is about the growing (up) of humanity, it is us that need to learn and become understanding parts of the whole. Maybe the cats and dogs as well as horses and other pets have seen this need and accompany us on our journey, presenting us with the chance to get to know ourselves and even get to love the person we are.The experience I gathered around the world, and my wish to support people in helping their pets and looking for ideas to create a better place in the world for animals, and indeed ourselves, formed the idea not only to write about common sense issues, explain some basic facts and include suggestions about natural products to guarantee better health for themselves and their animals, but also our spiritual connections.

You might read separate chapters about the physical, psychological and spiritual parts of all beings, but in reality, all is rolled in one. The physical can't exist without the spiritual and the energetic input, and vice versa, the physical brings the spiritual into earthly existence. The vibrational signature of every state we are in is different, so some parts of us are visible and others not, depending on how we are aware of energetic patterns and how much we see/perceive with our limited sight.

All there is on this earth, is interwoven, interdependent, in contact with and supporting one another, so the air around us must be filled with what we call vibrations, inundating all of the space between us, the animals, plants, the landscape, the planet and I believe the universe as well. This feeling of being in a 'sea of something' has been with me as long as I remember, especially being in a garden or forest. Certainly I wasn't aware of it all the time, day to day life, the ups and downs had to be dealt with and at times I got deeply involved in my own problems and setbacks, often getting the feeling of a discord, but as soon I was in nature amongst plants and animals the connection was back again. Maybe this is a novel idea to many of you and not everyone may see themselves as an integral part of the connection to animals and indeed, to the plants and the earth as well, but we now have the technology to prove what other cultures have said for thousands of years: we are all linked together. I dedicate a chapter on this subject.

Here is a bit more about my experience and what might have inspired me over the years to write this book and share my insights.

About 25 years ago, during some years living at a particular area I had several out of body experiences, (OBE's). One particular I would like to share because it explains my view on nature and how everything is ONE: I was taken out into space and in an instant I was far away from the earth but could see her as a globe in the distant, mostly blue in colour. Who took me there and how? I have no recollection; I was just transported in an instant. According to the famous Star Trek slogan: "Beam me up Scotty".

Looking around me I noticed I was standing on an balcony, definitely Greek in style with several tall columns and a balustrade made in the typical architecture of that country, spindles forming the bottom part, a rail connecting them on top. The funny thing was this balcony was only a triangular piece hanging there, glistening in white, against the backdrop of the black space. I can still picture it today. Then, I don't know how or from whom, I received the transmission right into my head of what actually means in words: 'look at the earth and know that all is connected, a web of many, of all kinds and shapes, intertwined in life and death, made up from the same basic materials.'

Looking back, I can see and understand now how it actually brought me to consciously realize my talents and gifts, of which I had not taken much notice before. There have been many people coming forward in the last few years, sharing their stories and experiences with OBE's or even NDE's (Near Death Experience), helpful and reassuring to all of us: We are definitely more than our physical body.

We are living in a world of the most dynamic change that we have ever seen or experienced in all of human history. And by all accounts, things will change more radically, unpredictably and faster in the future than they are changing in the present. The impact of change on every aspect of our life is something that we must take into consideration with every choice or decision that we make at every minute of our lives.

I enjoyed writing this book and offer it to you, so you may empower yourself and be a responsible and loving caretaker of your pet.

Contents

Preface 5

Introduction 9

Chapter One: The Physical and Physiological Part of Life 17

Chapter Two: The Psychological Part of Life 47

Chapter Three: The Spiritual Part of Life 59

Chapter Four: The Connection to All There Is 65

Chapter Five: Species Appropriate Diet 75

Chapter Six: Common Sense 103

Chapter Seven: Help for Self-Help 117

About the Author 147

Chapter One

The physical and physiological part of life

For many thousand years Nature/God/The Universe/The Creator or whatever it means for you, has tinkered with life, changed, eradicated and brought forth new organisms over and over again until they were like a finely tuned mechanism. Please excuse me using the word mechanism to describe this, I am aware it portrays the idea of a fixed and lifeless machine according to old ideas. But to our human mind it also describes precise workings and that is what I want to convey.

And what a marvel any organism is.

From a single cell amoeba to a more complex body of an animal, from the intricate composition of the soil to the wonderful life of plants, all is marvellously arranged and thought out to the minute detail. Everything on the planet is interwoven, interacts, cooperates, assimilates and excretes, multiplies and thrives according to the all governing plan of Nature.

Where does the information come from that tells each cell where its place is going to be in an organism and what it has to do there? Have the atoms that make up a cell an intelligence and know what function they should carry out? Liver cells make up a liver, heart cells get together to form a functioning heart and so on, isn't this amazing? Some amphibians grow new tails and even legs. There are many theories but let us just accept that fact and acknowledge that there is so much we do not understand as yet.

All organisms on this earth require certain substances to be healthy and functioning well, so what is or isn't in the diet, and indeed in our life, can make a big difference. As mammals we are all flesh, blood, and bone, however there are distinct differences between the species, mostly concerning the digestive tract. A horse needs an entirely different diet than a lion or a sheep, everyone needs specific nutrients and environment for its growth and wellbeing. It is termed a species appropriate diet, more in chapter 5.

Despite the differences in species there is a common wisdom regarding all life. Nature, over billions of years, has not only crafted the perfect interplay between all organisms and their food source, but has enlisted help to be able to process and assimilate food – bacteria. They are under the umbrella term micro-organism:

Micro-organisms are divided into six types: Bacteria, Archaea, Protozoa, Algae, Fungi, and Viruses. Each type has a characteristic cellular composition, morphology (means of locomotion), digestion and reproduction. Micro-organisms are beneficial in producing oxygen, decomposing organic material, providing nutrients for life and maintaining health. Some are pathogenic and cause diseases in plants, animal and human bodies, but are necessary to keep the balance.

A short explanation about viruses: A virus is a small infectious agent that replicates only inside the living cells of another organism. They cannot reproduce outside a host body. Viruses can infect all types of life forms, from animals and plants to microorganisms, including bacteria and can adapt and mutate.

Here, in this book, we are mainly concerned with bacteria, and to a lesser degree with fungi, specifically with mould. Bacteria are one celled micro-organisms that can live on their own, as parasites or as helpful agents in other organisms and are found everywhere. Of course, there are the 'baddies', some that can make us sick or even kill us, but the beneficial ones far outnumber the bad ones. The Yin and Yang of life. So all animal bodies, insects and even plants enlist a community of various microbes which help them function, and ideally, live in a symbiosis inside and outside of bodies. Only this symbiosis can assure our survival.

This is called the micro biome.

An example of beneficial bacteria are the ones important in the process of fermentation such as in wine and beer and baking (both are yeasts) and that of decomposition to produce soil from plant material in our compost heap. Other commonly known products are yoghurt, kefir and sauerkraut/fermented vegetable which are beneficial to us humans and ideally should be taken on a daily basis.

Probiotic (prolife) bacteria perform a wide variety of functions important for maintaining health and particularly improving and maintaining gut health. They are most helpful in treating constipation, diarrhoea and gas and bloating. Only a balanced and healthy intestinal micro biome can insure a strong immune system. Of course, *probiotic* formulas used by humans are developed specifically to fortify the bacterial species found in the human GI tract, however dogs and cats, as all other animals, have specific strains of bacteria unique to them and their specific diet.

A short explanation to *prebiotics*: they are a special form of dietary fibre, some water soluble and others water insoluble, both are important, which nourish the good bacteria (probiotic) in the gut. Therefore, it is important for us humans to include a variety of fibre rich vegetable and fruits.

One thing is for sure: our lives and even our identities are more closely linked to the microbial world than most people are led to believe. Hundreds of different kinds of bacteria work in unison to keep us healthy and it wasn't long ago when we began to uncover their valuable secrets. Scientific research says there is ten times more DNA of bacteria present in a human body compared to the DNA in human cells.

Are the bacteria having a human experience?

I am sure this would be true for other mammals as well. The importance of the micro biome in an organism has been ignored for a long time, but it is recognized now as one of the most critical part of any being. In reality this means we cannot separate our health from the wellbeing of the bacteria that lives in and on us. Living a life as nature intended, clean natural foods, clean water and a clean environment certainly supports a healthy life. Looking at our denatured food, contaminated water and environment, particularly the EMF fields from electronic gadgets, add to this our emotional stresses as humans (and this applies to domesticated animals as well), we can see how this paves the way for an interrupted life cycle and eventually ill health.

The lifestyle of humans, and this includes their pets, has been detrimental to our bacterial friends on whom we depend for many internal processes and external protection. Modern medicine has been fighting and killing them without looking at the consequences and have so altered the internal climate of many patients. The same can be said for the farm animals grown for meat which, down the line, are ingested by humans. Because of overuse of antibiotics (anti life) in the last 80 years or so, many bacteria are now resistant to them and stronger and stronger antibiotics have to be manufactured. Most people don't realize these kill all of the micro biome of a patient, good and bad alike, leaving the body's resistance to further infections wide open. Fortunately, the overuse of antibiotics has been recognized and should only be used in serious medical treatments and life-threatening situations. To make it more understandable I would like to explain this as follows: as any other life form on this planet, those bacteria want to survive and thrive, so they devised ways of becoming resistant and mutating, which we call the survival of the fittest. All organisms, in this case the bacteria, can communicate with each other and devise ways of survival, they mutate and become resistant to many of the antibiotics used. Viruses are not affected by commonly used antibiotics.

Prevention is always best

Nature wants us to take great care to establish a balance between the so called 'good' and 'bad' bacteria, not only within the body, but also through our thoughts and emotional expression which can favour positive or negative bacterial growth. We still do not completely understand the full impact of our bacterial flora on our health and physiology, but we are on the way. We certainly know the effects of the damage that is inflicted by a lack of good guys in our system.

Most of the immune system resides in the gut, therefore the majority of the bacteria living there must be the desirable ones in order to have proper digestion, good gut health and a strong immune system. These bacteria are easily damaged by GMO's (Genetically Modified Organisms: grains and plants), herbicides, pesticides, many other environmental toxins, emotional and physical stress and EMF's (Electro-Magnetic Fields) especially in the cities. Not many people take in account not only they themselves are affected by all of the above, including radiation from WiFi and appliances throughout the house, but their pets as well.

Much research has been done which shows that expressions like 'gut feeling' really have a leg to stand on. Thanks to many forward-thinking researchers we know now how the gut and brain is connected and how one influences the other. Especially the elderly benefit from taking care of and re-establishing the micro biome in the gut, which amongst other improvements in health, also helps to boost brain function and therefore a better life in older age. The immense number of cells which make up an organism exhibit such a cooperation and consideration amongst themselves, like a village where all inhabitants are concerned about their life together at any time of the day or night. But they also have a 'neighbourhood watch', warding off any intruders that are not welcome in the community.

> *This is called synergy, the community spirit of all the parts working towards the benefit of the whole entity.*

So far, we are all aware that the parts of a body are connected and work in synergy. But do we really think of its implications? Any organism always strives to run smoothly and stay balanced but should one part fail, other parts will take over until the sick part has recovered again and harmony can be restored. Every system needs energy to function; this is gained from outside the body in the form of air, water, food and sunlight and transformed via the breathing apparatus and digestion. The importance of sunlight will also be discussed later.

Communication processes are established between the organs and the organism as a whole, the electrical control mechanism and the immune system with its own data base to recognize friend or foe. Every cell relays its data via natural information channels using a constant flow of frequencies, photons (light quanta) and chemical messengers. All incoming impulses are analyzed, registered and recorded as either agreeable or not acceptable and will eventually cause symptoms/pain if the cause is not remedied. Many years ago, I read in a book this question of the author: "Who starts the first electrical impulse in a fetus?" This has intrigued me ever since, who indeed. Then another question arises: Who turns it off at that time we call death?

Here a quick overview how the Chinese see life. Of course, this concerns us humans, and can assist us in living a healthier and happier life, but why should animals be so much different? In Chinese Medicine we distinguish between **Jing, Shen** and **Qi**.

Jing is the essence that comes from the sperm/egg that has been given to us from our parents and is unique for each of us. It represents our constitutional component we are born with, similar to the DNA in Western understanding. This **Jing** cannot be replenished and when used up the organism dies, unless we learn certain rules governing life forces.

Shen is the mind/spirit which connects us to the God Force, the universe, the spiritual aspect of a being. This can be trained and improved through meditation and mindfulness.

Qi we call the vitality/energy of the body taken up by breathing, eating and drinking, but can be increased through certain exercises like Qigong, Tai Chi etc. as well. It is the active, motivating force not only of the cellular metabolism, but also of the electromagnetic and subtle energies that are circulated in the body, mostly via the acupuncture channels. This vitality results from the interaction of **Yin** and **Yang**. In a healthy body the constantly circulating **Qi**, in and out, up and down, is important for our wellbeing.

The increased unity of Jing, Shen and Qi guarantees a long and healthy physical life. When all 3 interact harmoniously, body, mind and soul are balanced, the individual is living not only a healthy life but also a happy one. But I firmly believe that we are not totally subject to this and can to some extend have an influence on our wellbeing depending what lifestyle and what outlook in life we decide on. As a matter of fact, it is now established that we can influence our genetic material via the lifestyle we choose, called Epigenetics.

Epigenetics means the study of changes in an organism caused by modification of gene expression rather than changes of the genetic code itself.

Genes are specific sequences of bases that provide instruction on how to make certain proteins, those proteins in turn trigger biological actions of various life functions. So, whatever we eat, drink, exercise, think, and this also affects aging, practically whatever we do in life will eventually turn on or turn off some of our genetic material. The genes we altered in regard of our lifestyle, i.e. stress, alcohol, smoking, bad foods and even living a life in fear like in a war time or natural disasters, can be inherited and be expressed by our descendants. We all carry more or less a residue of the experiences of our forebears and predecessors in us, experiences transferred into DNA through biological changes. The famous psychologist Carl Jung said we are all born with certain memories going back many generations, so I ask: is this similar in animals, specifically in pets whose parents had negative experiences in life?

My guess is this also concerns pets as well as humans, especially mistreated animals and a less than healthy lifestyle will have an effect on the offspring. This is not just expressed in physical ailments; the psyche of an animal may be affected as well and could vent itself in bad behaviour. In the physical department certain breeds of dogs, as well as some of those fancy cross breeds suffer from joint problems, hip dysplasia, osteoarthritis and other diseases because of in breeding; and also lack of nutrients and toxin overload in the parents.

It is up to us to make wise choices for a better and healthier lifestyle for the two- and four legged members of our family. Firstly, we need to be aware of the situation and by reducing emotional and mental stress as well as improving what we eat and a good lifestyle, gives us a chance not to be victim of our genetic material inherited from our ancestors. Our genes are not cast in stone, it is our choice to create health or ill health in our organism. So looking back to our ancestors, the life they lived and the stresses they might have gone through, like living through wars, might have turned on certain genes predisposing us to certain health issues. But today we have knowledge and facts and can learn how to turn it around.

Comparing the cleanliness of the canine genetics, originating from wild and in nature living wolves to our contaminated human genetics, I can see two different timelines going in opposite directions. Unfortunately, dog genetics are getting more contaminated through bad, de-natured foods, toxins, vaccinations and psychological influence from humans. Some humans have become aware that their lives, psyche and/or environment desperately need cleaning up. Many are taking the necessary steps to detox, physically and emotionally, turning off certain genes. Domestic animals cannot choose as they do in the wild, they are dependent on us. We have the responsibility to supply them with loving care and companionship, clean food and water and a nontoxic environment.

More than ever before, our bodies, humans and pets alike, need good nutrition, clean water and air and naturally a supportive environment for growth and wellbeing. The impact of change on every aspect of your life is something that we must take into consideration with every choice or decision that we make, may that concern nutrition, exercise, personal happiness, relationships, spiritual awareness and or respecting nature. At this point it is important to register the fact that our world we live in has never been as toxic in history of the planet before. There might have been many cataclysms, ice ages, floods and meteorites which wiped out many species and of course humans as well, but never before did we have so many manmade toxins poisoning all life on earth.

There are more than 80 000 manmade chemicals in use today.

Most are made from petroleum and range from highly toxic substances to less toxic ingredients in everyday products, which in a lot of cases are accumulative and difficult to be excreted by the organs. At the simplest level, a toxin is something capable of causing disease or damaging organs when it enters the body. This is important to understand as we discuss the role of dietary and environmental toxins in contributing to modern disease in humans as well as animals. Most of us won't get sick from eating a small amount of processed sugar, genetically altered cereal grain, industrial seed oil or inhaling poisoning fumes occasionally, but ingesting these most of our lives certainly has a detrimental influence on our health. Not only is the use of them harmful but so is the manufacturing as well as the disposing of them, causing more toxins. We also have to take in account common household items like soaps, creams, deodorants, perfumes, hair dyes, make up, aftershaves, toothpastes, washing powders, cleaners etc. leaving unhealthy residues in our body day after day.

Plastics are a curse of our time, not only leaching chemicals into foods, especially fatty foods, but also contaminating the earth and oceans where it enters into the food chain killing many animals who ingest the floating debris thinking it is food. The residue of plastics when breaking up is called micro plastic, found in all oceans and it is now a fact that the fish we eat is full of this. More of it later and how to use less of it. If we eat those manufactured foods and use the substances mentioned above daily and spend most of our lives in a unhealthy environment, the risk of developing chronic diseases rises significantly and will eventually alter our genes as discussed in *Epigenetics* above. This will be passed on to the next generation. Of course, the level of toxins in a body are dependent on the ability of organs to detoxify and at worst accumulate throughout a lifetime.

For pets the situation is not any different.

Vet clinics are overworked these days, pets are presenting with many diseases not heard of 20-30 years ago. Some more enlightened vets even offer a detox program for cats and dogs. Each generation of pets exposed to de-natured food, vaccinations, flea rinses and other toxic materials will be weaker than the one before. Sadly, with each sick animal there is money to be made. The emphasis is on building health rather than on fighting disease. Because it is difficult to be healthy in an unhealthy world, it is the responsibility of both physician and patient to create a healthier environment in which to live.

The basic needs of all organisms on earth are
Air, Water, Food, Sun Light and Sleep

Let us check out each item and discuss its importance for our physical and physiological health. Everyone knows without **air** we cannot survive more than a few minutes. We all enjoy going to the beach or the forest and immediately take a deep breath inhaling the ozone rich and fragrant air. What a relief! We are also taught different kinds of breathing techniques in yoga and similar modalities, and we learn that each breath inhaled and exhaled correctly, increases our energy level and also reduces stress levels. I am sure many have heard of breatharians, living entirely on the energy contained in the air and not taking any food for years.

Compare the air in cities and especially in industrial areas to a more natural part of our planet and there isn't much guesswork which is life giving and beneficial to all living beings. Air pollution poses a major threat to health and climate, to humans and pets alike. And let's not forget the all the other animals and plant life we so desperately need to survive. The alarming increase in pollution takes its toll generally while different pollutants have different health concerns. Respiratory diseases are rife in cities and industrial areas where air contamination is high, and we see many of the Asian population going about their daily business wearing masks.

Of course, not all pollutants are visible and come from a variety of sources. Most are from burning fossil fuels, like coal, petroleum and other combustibles, then there are the emissions from cars, trucks and airplanes and notably of many different kinds of industries all over the planet, many of them releasing toxic gases into the atmosphere. It does not help to point fingers; we are the customers. We absolutely need to look for other means to produce electricity instead relying still on coal and nuclear power which is the worst of all. The waste of the reactors will be highly toxic for many hundreds of years and no one has a solution except burying the waste in old mines, cementing it in or shipping it to so called Third World Countries. What a stupid idea to even contemplate.

Not to forget the emissions of methane of millions, or should I say billions, of domestic cattle and sheep, often packed in feed lots living a miserable life and mostly fed with matter foreign to the species. Even crops are affected by dirty air, so pollutants will be found in the harvested fruit, vegetable or grain. Adding to this the fumes from paints, carpets, furniture etc. in houses as well as fire retardants in soft furnishings, bedding and clothing, we come to understand the danger for everyone. Anyone that has bought a new car will know what I am talking about. The first few weeks one can only drive with the windows open, the outgassing of the plastics used in the interior is overwhelming, especially in hot weather. Anyone think this is healthy?

Sleeping on synthetic materials and inhaling those fumes for half of our lives cannot be beneficial. **Not only us, but our pets are exposed as well to plastic fillings in mattresses.** There are solutions for homes like air purifiers and certain plants that clean the air, also being diligent in using clean uncontaminated materials. Just to mention some of the plants that are said to help clean the air in a room: Mother in Laws Tongue, Peace Lily, Spider Plant, Rubber Tree and others. I am sure all plants are purifying the air to some extend but not all like to grow inside. The commercial air fresheners have manmade chemicals as scent and therefore not beneficial for humans or animals and very often cause allergies. Remember what goes into your lungs apart from clean air, needs to be detoxified again.

Something else we have to be aware of that should not be inhaled: the spores of mould as they can have a detrimental effect on health. There are many species of mould, penicillin is one of them and the hairs that grow on old bread, just as an example. Some cheeses have mould injected into them to give them a particular flavour, like blue cheese, gorgonzola, camembert and others which are not bad for us as humans if ingested. But mould and its spores should not be inhaled.

Do not confuse mould with fungi, mushrooms. They are related, but each has its own distinct characteristics, features and functions.

Living in a high rainfall area where moist air and the surroundings, like forests and other vegetation, carry the spores of mould can be a serious health concern. Mould is found outdoors in cut grass, compost piles and wooded areas and indoors in houses that are damp and not aired properly. It can grow on paper products, leather, furniture, carpet, air conditionings, just to name a few. These spores, if ingested or inhaled, can cause a range of unpleasant and even dangerous symptoms in humans and of course in your pets. We usually don't think of our pets being affected by them. They could even be more exposed being closer to mouldy floors or walls.

The reaction to mould spores can include nausea, vomiting, and, in severe cases bleeding in the lungs and nose. Anyone with asthma or allergies are more prone to be affected by them. Whether or not you're allergic to moulds, the exposure to it can still irritate your eyes, skin, nose, throat. Often homeowners are not aware of having mould in the house. It is advisable to check from time to time to keep the humidity low or use a de-humidifier, ensure adequate airing of rooms, and remove wet carpets.

Where **water** flows, we find life. After air, water is one of the second most important substance on earth and makes up approximately 70% of the surface of our planet and about the same in our bodies. All plants and animals must have water and cannot survive more than a few days without it.

If there was no water, there would be no life on earth.

Water has unique properties because of its polarity and the hydrogen bonds between its molecules, it is the perfect medium for transmitting substances into and out of a cell. A bit like a horse transporting a rider. Much research has been done especially in the last 30 years, uncovering other fascinating facts about water. There are many books and talks revealing the unique substance it is. It is the main solvent in an organism that transports many essential molecules and other particles around the body. These include nutrients in and waste products out from the body's metabolic processes.

A human body is made up of about 60% - 75% water, which forms the basis of blood, digestive juices, urine, perspiration and tears and is contained in lean muscle, fat and bones. Water maintains the health and integrity of every cell in the body and keeps the bloodstream liquid enough to flow through blood vessels. Interestingly about 70% of the earth is covered in water, coincidence? Most is saltwater about 95% of course, only a small percentage is fresh water but that is mostly locked up in ice. Good reason to not to waste any. As the body can't store water, we need fresh supplies every day to make up for losses from the lungs, skin, urine and faeces otherwise we face dehydration. The amount we need depends on our body size, metabolism, the weather, the food we eat and our activity levels. Inadequate fluid intake does not only cause dehydration but can increase the risk of kidney stones and urinary tract infections. It can also lower physical and mental performance and contribute to cognitive impairment in the elderly which we see often in retirement homes.

All chemical reactions in the bodies of mammals use water as a medium. From transportation to lubrication to temperature regulation and to acid - base balance (pH), water is just as important for pets as it is for all living organisms on earth. The amount varies depending not only what a dog is fed and the size of the meal, but also on the weather and to re-hydrate and cool down after exercise. Cats on the other hand can be a bit of a problem by not drinking much, they can be rather fussy about their water, so make sure it is fresh and the bowl cleaned daily. Just as with us humans, a pet's bodily function requires clean, uncontaminated and fluoride free water. Without adequate supply, the animal can become dehydrated and ill quickly. If living in the city, I suggest buying water in bulk for drinking from a natural spring - or have a good filter system which filters out many chemicals. Unfortunately, not everything is filtered out, many hormones, fluoride, pharmaceuticals and other toxins escape because of smaller molecule size. It pays out to invest in a more expensive filter, as the cheaper ones are not adequate.

Not only is the municipal water supply treated with chemicals to kill pathogens but in some countries fluoride is also added which is poisonous and NOT required for any bodily functions The idea about fluoride being necessary for good teeth has flown out the window some years ago. European countries do not add fluoride, it is declared a poison there. If you're interested, check independent sources and read the history of why fluoride was added to drinking water in the first place, and where it actually comes from, you will be surprised. Preferably spring water or filtered water should be offered to the pets as indeed it should be the choice of drinking water for ourselves.

Food
All organisms need nutrients to thrive, real foods from the earth. Over millennia, as the earth cooled and oceans and continents were formed, life also found its niches and slowly established itself. It emerged in so many wondrous and fabulous forms, shapes, colours and this planet became a place where all life forms became intrinsically connected and inter-dependent. This does not only mean providing nourishment for each other, but our flesh and blood will also nourish the earth when we become spirit again, we all get recycled.

Here I would like to point to something which has unfortunately become reality, especially in urban areas. Many humans are so contaminated by environmental toxins, pharmaceuticals and hormones that they are contaminating the soil in which they are buried in and may in turn contaminate the ground water. Most of the animals bred for consumption and even our pets getting more toxic every year. Cremation seems the best solution but even then, there are problems with heavy metals. In Sweden, the crematoriums have a special filter built in to filter out the mercury vapours from teeth fillings that are released at high degrees Celsius.

Our bodies want to heal and can - if we provide the proper nutritional foundation, clean environment and positive outlook.

Bodies are made up not only of flesh, blood and bones, there are numerous amounts of bacteria and micro-organisms in and on our body, most important for health and good functioning of the bodily system as a whole, as discussed earlier. More than ever our bodies and mind require good nutrition to combat not only stressful living but also the many toxins we ingest and come in contact with. Certain vitamins and other nutrients from fresh and unadulterated foods, like herbs, spices and vegetables have the ability to bind some of the toxins and remove them. Those wonder nutrients from plants are called phytonutrients and offered to us in all vegetables, especially in green plants like kale, broccoli, cabbage, any Asian greens, rocket, also in berries and many more fruits of course. All vegetables are beneficial, nature knows best.

I am sure everyone has heard of antioxidants. They are freely available as mentioned above, in the form of plants of all kinds, preferably organically grown, but also come in supplement form, for instance as Vitamins, Enzymes, Minerals etc. They help defend living cells from the damage caused by harmful molecules known as free radicals. These are unstable molecules and can harm cellular structures. Antioxidants donating electrons to the free radicals (the bad guys) and neutralizing them.

One of the body's protective mechanisms is to bind toxins in fatty tissue so as not to damage the organism as a whole. When dieting and losing fat too quickly, those toxins are released and may lead to a health crisis. Looking at many overweight pets these days, they would have a similar prognosis.

The key is to clean up our lifestyle and minimize more toxins coming in.

The food we ingest needs to be processed and absorbed properly within the body and this can be tricky for humans and pets in the time we live in. While good, natural and unadulterated food is still available, most food items on offer in supermarkets and other shops are processed to death and totally unsuitable for consumption, neither for humans nor pets. And not much good to the compost heap either.

In my profession as Naturopath, I would explain about processed and unnatural foods to my clients when they came for consultations. Some of them could see the point and would eventually do something about it. Some already knew but put it in the too hard basket. Others would try hard to avoid looking at the facts. When pressured, the knowledge about good, natural and basic human food is inherent in everyone. All but the most stubborn would agree there is much on offer to improve one's health. Strangely, when it comes to their pet's nutrition, common sense is often lacking. Sadly, the advertising industry has done a great job of brainwashing many pet owners to the detriment of the animals. It is time to let common sense reign.

Although many people have come to accept commercial foods as being normal to feed their dogs (and indeed themselves.) in fact, they are not. Nothing we produce commercially and artificially can ever rival the complex foods nature manufactured and perfected over millions of years, suited to each species. This includes us! All processed foods, for both humans and pets, whether sold in cans or packets are missing something that seems to be the most important nutrient of all. This key ingredient is something nutritional scientists have ignored so far, mostly on purpose because it cannot be patented, and money made from it. It is only found in freshly grown, uncooked whole foods and that is - *Life energy.*

Thanks to more recent science and research we now have a lot of technical data about vitamins, minerals, trace elements, enzymes, proteins etc. also can measure the energetic value in foods. Here I would like to clear up the myth of calories. All packaged foods have nutritional labels stating the number of calories as a guiding factor. The term calorie (cal) means a unit of energy required to raise the temperature of 1 gram of water by 1° Celsius. The calories you see on food packaging are actually measured in kg instead of gram (kcal) and were established in the 1800s by a chemist named Atwater. The original method was as follows: food was placed in a sealed container then immersed in water in an apparatus known as the bomb-calorimeter. The food was burned and the resulting rise in water temperature measured. What does that really mean? Even if two foods contain the same number of calories stated on the label, what is actually absorbed by the body varies with each person and type of food. The protein, carbohydrate or whatever is measured might have different values depending where its sourced from/grown. Every human or animal body will process nutrients slightly different, depending on their specific metabolism.

To me this system of counting calories could be at best an estimation, at worst it does not work at all. Especially anyone being aware of fresh and nutritious foods would be best not to rely on such a faulty system. While a few of the pet foods, and indeed human foods, certainly meet the criteria of vitamins and minerals and even essential fatty acids, these additives are often artificially manufactured and do not carry any life.

Looking at wolves, dingoes, and other wild dogs in their natural habitat we realize they are carnivores, and their food is raw meat, bones, organ meat and some of the fur or feathers. Interestingly they also eat the content of their preys' intestines which provides them with friendly bacteria. They are smarter than us. Meat eating animals mostly eat herbivores (grass eater) but will also eat omnivores (meat and grass eaters) and very occasionally other carnivores. The stomach and intestines of a herbivore prey contains their fermented meals and provides bacteria for digestion. As it is with the majority of supermarket food for humans the same seems to happen with pet food.

It only makes the purse of the manufacturer healthy.

Nutrition is the process in which substances in food are transformed into bodily tissue and provide energy. They are the building blocks for our body to grow and repair. One cannot build a house with faulty materials. For easy understanding of how we benefit from healthy food as nature intended, including what can go wrong in humans and in our pet's digestion - I will explain in quite general terms. The digestive tract begins in the mouth and ends in the anus. As soon as food arrives, or when one thinks of or smells food, the salivary glands in the mouth exude saliva, a digestive juice which moistens food, so it moves more easily through the oesophagus into the stomach. The same goes for dogs, think of the Pavlov Reflex. Saliva also has an enzyme that begins to break down starches in the food. After swallowing, muscle contraction (peristalsis) pushes the food down the oesophagus into the stomach. Gastric juices (mostly acid) break up the proteins in the food chemically and mechanically through churning/mixing. There is a reason why we have acid in the stomach. Not only to digest proteins and have them broken up into their components, but also to kill the unwanted bacteria coming in with the food or anything we have unconsciously swallowed.

The next step is the duodenum, there food is mixed with more digestive enzymes from the pancreas and bile from the liver. Digestive enzymes, as the name implies, breaks up the food particles and the bile emulsifies the fats.
Food is then squeezed into the lower parts of the small intestine, called the jejunum and the ileum. Nutrients are absorbed from the ileum, which is lined with millions of finger-like projections called villi. Each villus is connected to a mesh of capillaries, from there nutrients pass into the bloodstream. These villi provide a large surface and an exceptionally efficient absorption of nutrients and there again, more digestive enzymes are at work. After the nutrients are absorbed into the bloodstream and circulated in the body, the next step is the large intestine which removes water and finally moves the waste (faeces) into the rectum until they are passed out. We can picture the digestive tract like a conveyor belt moving the goods through the factory and each station has to do its job. If there is a problem on the first few stations it will cause a complication down the line. So, it is imperative to keep our digestion capabilities at a good level and take great care to feed ourselves only with natural and clean foods.

The gut is the interface between the outside and inside of an organism.

To recognize the different kind of mammals like herbivores, ruminants, omnivores and carnivores, we can look at their teeth and the motion of their jaws while eating. *Carnivores* have sharp incisors, the canine teeth, and move their jaws only up and down when tearing and eating. This helps them to catch and hold on to their prey, example are wolves, lions, and dogs and cats of course. In *herbivores* we find large molars more to the back of the jaw and they chew in a circular motion which grinds the grasses and leaves, like horses, deer etc. The *omnivores*, which means eaters of vegetable matter and meat, have both; large molars for grinding and sharp canines for holding on to meat, bears and chimpanzees are a good example. Then there are the *ruminants* presenting a digestive system that is totally different. They have several stomachs to ferment their food, usually grasses and leaves. The ones we are familiar with are cows and goats. *Please note,* this is a very basic explanation; there are many other differences in all species of animals and how they process their food.

The jury is still out on humans whether we are herbivores or omnivores. I see us as herbivores; this is because the length of our intestines is just right for digesting plant material, and we don't have canine teeth like chimpanzees. Someone who eats meat will probably say otherwise. We lack the enzyme to digest cellulose and only some of us have protease to digest meat. Looking at the various cultures on the planet, some survive mostly on animal protein and fat like the Innuits in a cold climate. Other cultures living in rainforests for instance, are based mostly on plant material. Eating insects is another way of getting protein apart from meat, uncontaminated by hormones, antibiotics, pesticides etc. I would recommend it. Just recently I read an article by an anthropologist who, by examining bone, DNA and human faecal matter from ancient human sites, concludes that our ancestors have been eating mostly plant material. Furthermore, fossilized microscopic plant foods were found all over those sites, pointing to a vegan diet. My guess is that we are creatures who have adapted to eating what nature provided in different parts of the world. Obviously, this would have happened over thousands, maybe millions of years.

Here we are concerned with the carnivores in our care, what to feed our furry friends, and what is appropriate for their particular digestive tract. Even so, they are flesh, blood and bone like us, their intestinal tract and nutrient requirements are different. Their teeth, gut and digestive physiology strongly support this. Most people don't spend a lot of time thinking about their own digestive processes, much less on the workings of their animal's digestive system. It usually boils down to thinking about feeding times and letting them out to go to the toilet when they need to. But what does and does not happen in their digestive tract from the time their food enters their mouths, and until the waste is excreted is most crucial. This process in between requires the right gastric juices, hydrochloric acid, enzymes and bacteria, as well as a good motility (churning) of stomach and the intestines, to get the best out of the food. This certainly depends on the quality of what is fed.

The carnivorous diet (raw meat) goes through a very effective digestive process, which occurs in a relatively short gastrointestinal tract. Dogs and cats (like other carnivores) have a significantly shorter tract compared to other non-meat eating (herbivorous) animals, whereas humans have a medium length tract. The relative length of the gut reflects the nature of the diet, and how efficiently or slowly the food is broken down and absorbed. Fresh, raw meat is easily digested and absorbed compared to vegetable matter; carnivores have a short gut, and rapid gut transit time. Fresh meat can be digested and processed in the carnivore's GI tract in as little as 8-12 hours. Plant and vegetable material in a herbivore's gut can take 3-5 days to be processed, which is more like a fermentation. Hence the smelly, bulky faeces and intestinal gasses of some animals.

This highly acidic environment in the stomach of canines favours the breakdown of raw meats and bones, into soft digestible material. The low pH, much more acidic than humans, is also extremely effective at killing bacteria, particularly potentially pathogenic bacteria often present in rotten meat. Dogs are *scavenger carnivores*, eating what they find; cats are what's called *obligate carnivores*, which means they are true meat eaters and cannot survive on plant material, despite what you read on tins or packaged food. As scavenger carnivores, dogs can survive to some extent on plant material, but they will not thrive. If the stomach acid is diminished, the protein cannot properly be broken up in its components. This poses a lack of nutrients to the overall health of an animal. This applies to us as well, especially when we get older.

Most people are aware of *gastro-oesophageal reflux disease* (GERD) and other complications of improper digestion. I would like to clear something up that has been a misunderstanding for a long time, years actually. While most people think that reflux occurs because of an overproduction in stomach acid, it's actually the opposite. In most cases, it is due to having low amounts of stomach acid that leads to this problem. Reflux occurs when the contents and acid from the stomach flow back into the oesophagus. The reason for this is the valve between the stomach and the oesophagus not closing properly. Caused by a weakening of the tissues of the valve, and of course inappropriate foods and drink, but stress is mostly the culprit.

Nowadays we hear similar reports from vets about gastro-oesophageal reflux disease in pets, as described on the previous page. The scenario is similar to human complaints of low stomach acid resulting from all kinds of stressful situations. Foods not designed for a particular animal and also late-night feeding can pose a problem. As we get older, we often don't have an adequate amount of stomach acid. Causes can be chronic stress, nutrient deficiencies, smoking, bacterial infections, medications etc., therefore the diet should be changed, or natural supplements taken to increase this acid. For many years the medical establishment thought indigestion was caused by too much acid and solved this by prescribing acid blockers, making the complaint much worse.

Practising holistic medicine and using iris diagnosis to verify the level of stomach acid has been helpful to say the least. It is certainly especially helpful to clients to get them off antacids. Everything depends on a healthy, well working digestive apparatus to assimilate the nutrients from food.

Let the sun in.
Without the sun's heat and light, the Earth would be a lifeless ball of ice and rock. Ancient cultures worshipped the sun, they knew of its importance for survival and good health. The sun warms the seas which causes the water to evaporate and falls down as rain, it creates earth atmosphere, generates the weather patterns and keeps the earth and other planets in our solar system in their place by gravity forces. Solar flares have been known not only to interrupt physical life on the planet but also influence our psyche. Imagine this sunlight travelling for so many millions of kilometres through space and giving us life. The earth is fortunate to be in the 'Goldilocks' zone of our solar system, not too close and not too far away from its life source, just the right distance to support all creatures, great and small.

The sun radiates energy equally in all directions; the earth intercepts and receives part of this energy. For us, the visible light contains the spectrum we see as a rainbow after rain. It is really an optical illusion as the light coming from the sun hits droplets of water and gets refracted (bent) and reflected at different angles which we see as the particular colours. UV rays (tanning), infrared (heat), radio waves (communication) are also important part of the sun's rays as are others we are not concerned with here. Humans can actually see only a fraction of the whole spectrum in comparison with some animals that can even see UV radiation.

Light travels in waves and is the only form of energy visible to the human eye.

Most life forms have evolved to capture and use this energy for various purposes pertaining to their species. Plants use sunlight to create food and oxygen for humans and animals called photosynthesis. During photosynthesis in plants, the light energy is captured and used to convert water, carbon dioxide and minerals into oxygen and mineral rich organic compounds. It would be impossible to overestimate the importance of photosynthesis in the maintenance of life on earth. There is a theory that the plants over millions of years enriched the air with oxygen to later sustain life as we know it; prepared the atmosphere for us as mammals. If photosynthesis ceased, there would be hardly any food for us to eat, except perhaps for mushrooms, they do not require sunlight to grow. They have a different mechanism for survival. Additionally, the various minerals and trace elements necessary for health would not be available unless plants have processed them first into smaller molecules, so they are in an acceptable size for our digestive system.

As mentioned above, photosynthesis also uses up carbon dioxide and gives us oxygen. Forests are a great source, as oceans are and the green masses of plants covering the planet. So, planting trees everywhere should be on top of our to do list and clear-felling forests just to make room for more cattle should be punished severely. Carbon dioxide is taken up by plants, the soil and the oceans, it does not cause any climate change. The body is designed to manufacture the vitamin D3 it requires by producing it when our bare skin is exposed to sunlight and then stored in fat cells. D2 is found in plant foods and the D3 only in oily fish, egg yolk and unpasteurized milk. Vitamin D3 aids the uptake of calcium necessary for bone growth and strength and can also be taken as supplement, especially in winter in the northern hemisphere. I would suggest a supplement for the majority of people in cities these days.

Our ancestors lived outside all year round, but in our so-called modern world the majority of people live and work indoors. Like other organisms we have the capability to manufacture specialized proteins that transform light energy into chemical energy. One of these proteins in the eye, and now thought to be in the skin as well, known as *melanopsin*, uses light energy to set our biological clock. As much as day and night is important for all life on earth, so is sunlight. All creatures are woven into earth cycles and in humans we call it biorhythm.

Biological rhythms are the repeating cycles of activity which occur in living organisms. The best-known example is the daily circadian rhythm, which represents the cycle of day and night. Bathed in strong lights at night, watching TV and computer screens until late throws this biorhythm out of balance and not only affects physical health but also our emotional stability. People deprived of their natural sleep cycle have more accidents and are stressed more often. We know from studies of shift workers, they are more prone to health problems by going against the natural rhythm, not only affecting physical health, but also concerning moods and emotions. As much as this day and night rhythm is important so is the energetic cycle for all internal organs. All organs reach their peak and low within 24 hours. This natural rhythm allows the body to do 'housekeeping', an internal cleaning and self-care of all organs, it also plays a role in hormone production, body temperature and brain activity.

Different animal species have different bio rhythms according to the life they lead. For instance, it would be quite a different cycle for nocturnal species. So, I surmise that pets have their good and bad days, just like us - depending on their biorhythm cycles. In certain environmental situations, (human made of course) pets would experience similar problems, and their particular biorhythm might be affected as well. Having low lights or putting them in a darker corner of the house at night might be the answer to keeping their biological cycle intact.

These days, we are warned not to go out in the sun, so many people spend their lives indoors. They often travel in a car or bus from home to workplace and back. On the weekends, they might a few hours in nature but mostly to the shopping centre or fitness centre - indoors again. Everyone is told to slather themselves with sunscreen to block out the life-giving sunlight, and many people don't research the contents of those creams. They contain foreign chemicals which are burned and absorbed into the skin and bloodstream, burdening our liver as a de-toxifying organ, even more. Most skin cancers appear on places of the body usually covered by clothing, so there must be other reasons as well why we are affected by it. Another downside of sunscreens is the contamination of lakes and beaches with unknown effects on marine ecology. It is now studied how sunscreens release different compounds, trace metals and inorganic chemicals, into seawater and harming not only the myriad of fish, but also the corals and other sea plants. It affects the Mediterranean significantly, because of the smaller body of water and the high number of holiday makers from all European countries. Surely, looking at the many visitors to the Great Barrier Reef, there would be a negative effect as well. I would like to add the toxicity of make ups, deodorant, soap residue, perfumes, after shave, hair dyes and such like affecting sea life just as much.

Light is energy

Light brings energy in the form of heat and as we learned earlier, energy never gets lost, it just changes form. Most life forms have evolved to capture and use this energy for various purposes. Plants have developed the ability to use energy from light to build complex sugars. Though humans can't do this, we have evolved other impressive skills that involve sunlight, manufacturing Vitamin D3 in the skin is definitely one of them, as mentioned above. Neither animals nor plants can live without vitamin C, and it is therefore surprising that some animals (some fish and birds, and a few mammals including guinea pigs and humans) have lost the capability to produce it over the course of evolution. Fortunately, dogs and cats have the enzyme to manufacture vitamin C.

In the human eye there are specialized cells with light sensitive proteins. These cells are known as rods and cones and make us get out of bed when light enters the eye. Certain parts of the brain are stimulated by receiving sunlight through the eyes and so the sun plays a vital part for health and also keeping us happy. I bet everyone would agree going out into the sunshine lifts any negative mood.

*All organisms on this planet evolved **without** sunglasses.*

We certainly should protect eyes in dazzling snow or when out on the ocean to counteract the strong reflection of the water. However, wearing sunglasses on a permanent basis when outdoors, or using them as a fashion statement is actually detrimental to our wellbeing. Letting the sunlight into our eyes early morning and evening when the sun is closest to the earth, has been done by cultures living thousands of years ago. It is called sun gazing. The sun helps brain function, which can improve the nervous system, hormonal regulation, muscle function, immune health, and carries many other benefits as we have discussed.

Here I would like to add more information about the effect of **colours** on the body, and certainly on the mind. Nature is full of colours and we all respond to it, physically and emotionally. It is commonly known how the colour blue relaxes and calms us, and greens, like the many different shades in nature soothes our minds. We have favourite colours, which might change throughout our lives and even dress to suit our mood. It is the frequency of each colour that can soothe, balance, or energize the body when we look at it. Even blind people can 'feel' colours, this confirms the fact that colours have vibrations. The colours of the rainbow are also associated and resonate with our energy centres, the Chakras.

The knowledge of body-mind-spirit and how they are woven together came to the west from the classical Chinese Medicine, especially in the last hundred years. They attributed colours to the organs, for instance green to the liver, red to the heart, yellow to the spleen and stomach, black to the kidneys and white to the lungs. Today we have modalities like Colour Therapy, which is a holistic, non-invasive treatment of applying certain coloured lights to acupuncture points or pain areas to increase or decrease the energetic balance in the body or alleviate pain.

The Colour Therapy I have been offering in my clinic was called Colour Puncture. A rather unfortunate name but making sense in regard of using the acupuncture points on a person. I had amazing experiences with this therapy, one particular one stands out. A patient was experiencing an asthma attack brought on by essential oils; they were severely choking and gasping for air - the situation looked very serious indeed. Luckily, I had my colour therapy pens handy and immediately applied blue on the appropriate acupuncture point, the relief was instant.

Different species see colours differently from humans, depending on the make up of their eyes, specifically the number of cones in the back of the eye. Dogs have less cones than humans, so it is assumed they see colours but not as bright and less shades. Somehow this makes sense because their most important sense is smell and not sight as it is for us. With cats it is different, they see better in darkness than dogs or humans because of more light sensitive rods in the back of the eye. They are equipped for hunting in the night. Just because animals can't see the colours as we do, (which is still an assumption), they definitely respond to Colour Therapy. If you remember colours are frequencies, so each colour with its specific wavelength applied to the body does affect animals similar as us. Red to energize, blue to calm, green to balance and yellow and orange are happy colours.

We touched on sleep earlier, but I would like to recap as it is essential to get enough quality sleep each night. It is an important part of our daily routine and just as vital to our survival as food and water. Sleep patterns and lengths change as we get older. Babies sleep 16-18 hours a day which may boost growth and development, for school children it would certainly be best to sleep at least 8-9 hours. The hours decrease to 7-8 in adults, but in general people often get less sleep due to their work schedule, TV and internet entertainment round the clock or other activities. Many people are affected at some stage of their lives with insomnia, this could be age or health related, triggered by worries and anxiety, and of course unhappiness.

Our brain forms new pathways in sleep, creates new memories storage, practically restores physical and mental wellbeing, hence long-term sleep deprivation is associated with increased risk of ill health. It is important to note that the brain also detoxifies during sleep. Even so, we do not fully understand sleep, it is beneficial for almost every type of organ system, immune function and can increase disease resistance. Restful sleep certainly paves the way to a happy morning. A small percentage of the population needs less than 5 hours a night and can still be highly productive, manage to function and are generally not tired when awake.

Healthy and good sleep rejuvenates our bodies when we get older.

Sleep really is a complex process. We have clinics researching what is actually happening when we go through several stages until the REM (rapid eye movement) sleep. It is said that we dream mostly in the REM sleep but, not all of us remember them. In dreams, we tackle issues from our waking lives. Trying to resolve them during sleep can take on a surrealistic feeling and cause weird images to appear in our dreams. Sometimes we act out scenarios which wouldn't be possible in real life. Occasionally we experience an incredible dream and often ask ourselves what it could mean. We can train ourselves to recall dreams by keeping a diary handy to write it down soon after waking up. The longer we wait before writing them down, the faster the memory of the dream goes up in 'smoke' like a ghost.

I believe some dreams are not superficial, they have meaning as some people can verify. They can be premonitions, downloading creative ideas, solutions to a problem or a journey out of the body. The veil between worlds might be very thin when we sleep, grant us a chance to slip through and connect with other dimensions, other beings or even get in touch with the spirits of our relatives or ancestors. Sleeping removes us from our preconceptions, our acquired ideas and mindset and sets us free to experience what we would not dare to do and think in real life. We still have to unravel the mysteries of sleep. Animals sleep and dream as well. Horses very often sleep/rest standing up, especially when younger. This makes sense as they are flight animals and have to be ready to run off if attacked. Even fish have rest periods, I don't think there are any animals that don't sleep. I recently saw a video of an octopus that went through sleep cycles similar to ours and changed its colours, maybe this indicates they are dreaming too, and why not?

Our pets do sleep a lot and they definitely dream as well. Dogs sleep at least 12 hours of the 24-hour day and cats a lot more. They are going through similar cycles as humans, which we notice by the way they slow their breathing becoming more regular. When the rapid eye movement (REM) begins, it is a sign they are dreaming. We often hear them growling, making all kinds of noises, moving paws as if running and even their facial muscles tremble. I bet they dream about playing with their toy, chasing a ball or another animal (this might depend on what kind of breed they are.) and probably process their day to day experiences just like we do. The closeness and their attachment to humans might even increase their dream potential and, who knows, they might even dream about how we smell.

Cats are night animals, they can fall asleep, anywhere and in any position for up to 20 hours a day. But why do cats sleep so much? For thousands of years, they have hunted at night and have generally been most active between dusk and dawn. Although they are domesticated, they still have the genes a hunter needs. They love to spend time at night playing and if possible, going on a prowl to the dismay of their humans. All this hunting and stalking requires a lot of energy, so they sleep most of the day. Fortunately, many adjust their schedules to tie in with you, play and cuddle up on the couch with you when home. They can be observed to have similar sleep stages and certainly twitch their tails and whiskers and run in their dreams, like the dogs. Some of their rest time is spent dozing - they are sleeping but are still alert enough to perceive prey or danger. They are awake and alert within a moment's notice - a perfect hunter.

It is said **laughter** is the best medicine and this should be taken seriously. A good belly laugh is literally the cheapest form of therapy. It lifts the spirit, can help heal the body and improves the immune system, stimulates the heart and lungs, increases blood flow and also triggers the release of endorphins, the feel-good hormones. Many studies have proven that ill people heal faster and are in a better and more positive mood. Lucky for us it is contagious.

Why do we do it? It seems a natural relaxation response with the added bonus of providing a massage to the internal organs and toning abdominal muscles. I suppose it makes sense calling it a belly laugh. We love the feeling of a shared laugh, it makes us feel safe, can diffuse tense feelings and aggressiveness and it fosters closeness with others. As soon as someone starts giggling, we get infected; needless to say, it is especially healing when shared in a group of friends. Life can be funny, but it needs discernment, not laughing at people, but laughing with them.

Some years ago, someone had the idea to start laughter yoga where people come together and just sit around and laugh. These days, there are workshops available for companies to build trust and team spirit amongst the employees, reduce their stress and improve the ability of coping with challenges. One study found that laughter has a positive and sustained effect on workplace wellbeing. I would like to suggest that everyone should break out into laughter on a regular basis. I certainly watch or read funny sketches just about daily, I find it counteracts the not so perfect world we live in.

Use your smile to change the world; don't let the world change your smile.
Chinese Proverb

Even smiling is contagious and can transform a situation. Don't we feel we can't help but smile back when someone smiles at us? It certainly makes us more attractive and lifts our mood. Smiling amazingly exercises most our facial muscles, which in turn will send happy messages to the brain. Those brain chemicals aid in calming one's nervous system and have a calming influence on our heart rate and blood pressure, very similar to laughter. A smile, even when faked is helpful; the right muscles are used so the brain gets the message anyway. We can't always control things happening in our lives but smiling and laughing more often can certainly change our interior climate for the better and help others to lighten up. Fake it until you make it, is certainly good advice in this regard. Some say smiling is unique to humans, but when we observe some primates, we notice they appear to bare their teeth in a friendly gesture as well. It could be taken for a snarl, but once we look closely we recognize the different set of their jaws and teeth and realize it resembles what we would call a smile, and could be meant to appease others, pacify a situation. It seems the primates know when the situation arises to smile at others, wanting to be liked.

Do dogs smile? It certainly looks that way. They open their mouth, pull up the upper lip and expose their teeth, some even have their tongues lolling out. It is in a soft and relaxed way they open their mouths, compared to a snarl when there is facial tension, a stark difference. It seems some breeds are more of a happy go lucky type and show a more pronounced smile. The feeling I get from a smiling dog is that they want to be social and tell us they are happy. Tail wagging certainly lets us know they are happy but smiling seems to be more of a distinct sign of happiness, it seems to be addressed to us specifically because they look us in the face and keep eye contact. It may have developed as a result of the dog-human relationship over thousands of years and gives us an opportunity to study communication between species. There is so much to learn. Who knows, the dogs might even mimic us.

THE THREE AMIGOS

Chapter Two

The psychological part of life

Leadership through Relationship
In this chapter I would like to discuss the fact that the human psyche very often controls the psyche of the pet. I am talking here about a most important issue concerning our pets; the way the animal takes on our emotions and feelings and very often our illnesses and symptoms as well. More and more people beginning to realize the bond they have with their pet, and the responsibility they have to live up to. It is becoming more widely accepted that animals (plants as well and I believe any matter on this planet really), have their own consciousness, their particular understanding of the world and themselves.

Pet relationships are important and the key to having a happy, healthy pet is to be a responsible parent who constantly strives to make the pet's life a good one. Equally important is to be a good leader, setting limits, keeping them safe and taking care of their physical and social needs. Pets in turn will be great companions, looking after our safety and being there for our social comfort. Happily listening to our problems without interrupting or judging, always unconditionally loyal and loving - no wonder they are called man's best friend.

For hundreds of years, accepted scientific thought has categorized animals as lower on the evolutionary scale with less complex brains, and therefore incapable of thoughts, feelings and purposes. Now more people have come to accept that animals have a language of their own, show emotions and a potential for thought processes. The progress with recognizing this appears to be really slow. It seems a big hurdle for humankind to overcome and finally regard animals as conscious beings. Beings that have the same right as humans to live their lives in a decent manner on this planet.

As mentioned earlier, it was generally believed that the body works as a machine whose parts would inevitably break down and be repaired until worn out. Unfortunately, it is still mostly the case in modern medicine, body parts get replaced or fixed up rather than looking at and removing the cause of the particular breakdown. Needless to say, taking care of and mending body parts is lifesaving in accidents. We certainly have outstanding technology available in emergency wards taking care of victims of disasters, car accidents etc. There is also a high standard in manufacturing prosthesis for limbs. This technology is also used to help pets when injuries occur, for example when a pet is hit by a car or any other incidents. Regrettably more and more dogs are having implants because joints are worn, riddled with arthritis, needing hip replacements and spinal surgery. Does that mirror the downward spiral of human health?

Treating illnesses and diseases clearly needs another approach. Having taken interest in my clients' history over years, and indeed having looked at myself, I have learned that there is always an underlying cause for the dis-ease, often emerging only after months or years. Those causes must be discovered first and foremost before a person, or an animal can recover. Research has shown that many human diseases and afflictions stem from our emotions, may that be anger, fear, guilt, grief, embarrassment, loneliness etc. Our pets tune in and can eventually display similar behaviour and illnesses.

Symptoms of discomfort or pain are the body's signs that all is not well and needs attending to. The origin of symptoms occurs on many levels, including the physical, mental-emotional, and also the spiritual. As it happens, we are emotional beings. Anger, fear, jealousy, shame and grief releases damaging chemicals via our thinking and subsequently creating a stress situation in the body. Trauma of any kind can contribute to illness, festering after many years when the original cause is often consciously forgotten, but still lingers within the subconscious level. A certain trigger might set the trauma free which presents the opportunity to either deal with it or to deny it. If not dealt with, it will possibly rear its head again at some stage later. Even perceived danger causes stress.

Illness, physical or emotional, does not occur without cause and might have originated many years before.

Therefore, a person must be seen as a whole, involving a complex interaction of physical, spiritual, mental, emotional, environmental and social factors and diagnosed and treated with a personalized approach. One important realization is that our pets also have an emotional life. When they are surrounded by stressful situations over time, these negative energies accumulate and build up in their bodies, creating dis-harmony and stress, just as with us humans. Observing the pet integrated in its social setting is a start to recognize the cause of the behaviour or physical complaint.

Because we are their family, pets especially when young, take on our habits and emotions, which can be as detrimental to their health as it to ours. As small children, we copy our parents because they are our only reference point at that stage in life. Unfortunately, it is seldom recognized that when we get older those habits do not suit us as well when grown up or as they did our parents. This scenario was lifesaving for people who grew up in a tribal situation thousands of years ago; it guaranteed survival in the wilderness. The dogs that accompanied humans in those days lived off their spoils from hunting, and probably acted as watchdogs as well. They were free to come and go and followed the tribes when it suited them, humans and animals both profited from the relationship.

Today, everything has changed, we are not hunters anymore. Sadly, we have become supermarket foragers, led by advertising, someone else's opinion. It is time to realize we cannot afford to live in a thoughtless manner anymore, especially regarding the lives of pets, our immediate environment and indeed all inhabitants of this planet. Often, we subconsciously acquire a pet to fulfil our needs. Sometimes as a watchdog, companion, or plaything. Other times it might be as a replacement when a loved one passes away, or a relationship ends. This often reflects the dreams we have about ourselves as well as our perceived needs. In some cases, this does not only reflect our wishes about ourselves but, subconsciously we pick animals similar to our own looks and behaviour. Much can be said about a person regarding their choice of a pet.

Don't we joke about a man that looks like his bulldog or the poodle that displays nervous and fidgety behaviour, just like the lady on the other end of the leash. I am sure we all have seen people and pets that grow alike in looks and manners. With so many different breeds to choose from to suit the lifestyle of individuals or families, health and fitness, young or old, it isn't difficult to welcome the right type of pet into our home. Birds are also lovely companions when kept according to their needs, bond with people, are easier to look after and don't need walks.

Sitting across clients in a clinical situation I found it helped them to relax and be comfortable when I mirrored them in behaviour. For example, using similar language patterns, similar arm and leg movements and even aligning the breath which can help to calm an excited and worried person. These are conscious actions to help others, we call it empathy. We thought for a long time that this behaviour was just reserved for humans and maybe primates, but apparently pets seem to have empathy as well. It is empathy that enables us to smile or laugh when chatting to a friend, spontaneously responding to and mimicking their facial expressions and movements.

Pets love to please by mimicking behavioral patterns of their humans, and as we heard before animals do not make a distinction of negative or positive, they just copy. Being social animals living in groups and families, they might mirror our troubles as well, such as anxiety or negativity. They may even get a similar illness, so we have a chance to see ourselves in their mirror and turn things around. Loving cats and dogs can certainly help us cope with life's stresses. I think we are now becoming fully aware how they enrich our life, and how important they have become as a calming friend and relaxed companion. It is also true for horses.

Pets are likely to mirror the person they have bonded with.

Dogs are naturally good communicators using visual, olfactory (smell), and vocal clues, they are masters at reading another dog's body language as well as that of humans. Some people question if they are responding emotionally like we do, or if they are just imitating our actions or that of their dog friends without being aware. They might not be able to speak our language because of a lack of certain physical parts pertaining to speech, but they definitely can feel our vibrations. I believe, and many dog and cat lovers will agree, we tune into each other and read subtle cues about stress level, moods and good and bad vibes. Pets often will try to give you a nuzzle when one is sad or crying. They certainly have feelings and also detect feelings in others.

Through mirroring, we have an opportunity to recognize and become aware of our own issues through what is expressed by our companion animal. Of course, none of us can always be well adjusted and not fall prey to the crazy (and toxic) world around us at some stage in our lives. The sooner we acknowledge a problem, help arrives at our doorstep presenting us with solutions for ourselves and the pets dependent on us. Lifestyle changes can create stress in both humans and animals. Moving to a new house, death or birth, a new relationship or new pets in the house can all cause stress. In humans, stress tends to manifest itself physically as muscular tension, endocrine balance and change in metabolism, which eventually lowers the immune function. We know now that stress appears in a very similar manner in animals. It can lead to organ dysfunction, lowered immune response, disturbed sleep patterns and altered behavior. They cannot reason about a new situation or loss of affection and are at our mercy.

Here is something to think about: Organs renew themselves after a certain time span. We are a new person every few years, why is it then that we carry the same illness over many years or even a lifetime? The information from own and inherited experiences present in each cell gets transferred into the new tissues. This eventually presents the same dis-ease in the 'new' body unless we become conscious of it and pay attention, only then is it possible to 'ease the dis-ease'. It is the same information that we, via our emotion of anger, fear, hate, grief etc., often created in the first place, always affecting the weakest part of our bodies presenting us with pain or a symptom.

We are electrical beings

Every living function, whether it is conscious or unconscious, physical or mental, is powered by low levels of electrical current. When we think about it a little more, it starts to make sense. Perception of pain, muscle contraction and movement, nerve function, glandular secretions, healing and regeneration, and brain activity are all electrically driven functions of the body. Think about the heart, the most dominant component of the human body. The heart is a muscle and contracts by low levels of electrical current; it can be monitored and measured with an EKG. It generates the largest electromagnetic field in our body, greater than the field of the brain. It is not only an organ pumping oxygenated and nutrient rich blood through the body, evidence shows the heart also plays a greater role in our mental, emotional and physical processes than previously thought in the western world.

The Chinese, and their acupuncture therapies can teach us much about the fact that we are electrical beings; and that each organ has its own meridian or channel in which the energy moves freely or at times gets blocked. The heart channel for instance has points which can be treated for emotional upsets to restore balance and encourages the body and mind to heal. Many other cultures have held the heart in high esteem and knew of its powerful aura. More research will be required to determine the nature and function of this energy/information field the heart sends out and as we are all aware, touches others, may they be human or non-humans. The world would be a different place if everyone chose to think and act from the heart.

The *Heart Math Institute* teaches us about the intelligence of the heart and their website is a great place to gain more information on how we can influence our daily lives with heart felt thoughts, like practicing forgiveness, spreading kindness and compassion, especially for the ones that suffer from our human thoughtlessness. They also have tools available for reducing stress, empowering oneself as well as contributing to the *Global Coherence Initiative*. This is an international endeavour to bring together the hearts of humanity and promote peace and their ongoing research on the interconnection between humanity and Gaia, our earth.

Let's start now and send out vibes from a loving and kind heart to all beings.

The last few years has seen a tremendous amount of research into the brain. As we discussed earlier, this organ is closely connected to our digestion (or the lack of it), so it is wise to eat clean and nourishing foods to start with. This might not be easy for everyone, especially having taken little interest in keeping the body healthy, it means to change ones' thoughts first of all. Unless our mind is in tune what we should change we will fall back on old habits. Keeping one's body healthy is a conscious undertaking.

To change behaviour is to change thinking, here is an explanation that might help to encourage different thought patterns: Just imagine a path in fields or forest that is used regularly, it will become what we term: a well-trodden path. The same happens in our brain, same or similar thoughts create pathways of nerve connections which keep those thoughts alive, beneficial or negative. Like the song we hum over and over again and cannot wipe from our mind. Because the way we think affects everything in our lives, it is wise to make an effort to change, acquiring beneficial thoughts as well as habits. To adopt a new behaviour takes a conscious effort, intention and thoughtful process. Fortunately, our brain is capable of change (at any age), until we die.

This is called neuroplasticity.

Clean and nourishing thinking, exercising new thought processes, learning something new that is of interest, good sleep and many more things can be done to grow new neurons (brain circuits). It does not matter how old we are, the brain as well as other organs, can regenerate again. Remember: you don't use it you lose it. Physical exercise keeps the blood flowing and removes waste from the brain which improves clarity, memory and attention span. Getting to know oneself and being able to see life more clearly, eases the path to change one's perception. It helps us to become more sensitive of our influence on our surroundings. Naturally, this includes other people and our environment, but it affects the pets more so as they are especially susceptible to it, because they want to please.

As soon as we have good brain function and a happy heart, we are clearer about our lives, and have less emotional hiccups, therefore we are easier to 'read' by our furry companions. When we are open and tune in to the animal, our brains are synchronized with theirs. I think this would be possible with any animal, provided we are in a quiet state of mind, showing respect and gratitude. There are a few amazing human beings able to do this out in the wild, but only a handful. I have trained horses easily and effortlessly by 'unzipping' myself and showing the real me, a trustworthy friend asking for a favour. Although dogs are remarkably well-adapted to living with humans in human environments, we must also acknowledge that human environments can be stressful for dogs. We have to allow them be dogs and not turn them into 'little humans' because we lack company. I personally resent the idea that some people compare the mental capacity of dogs to 4-5-year-old children. Animals are different in their make-up; they are not children. Therefore understanding one another's view of the world helps strengthen the bond between you and your furry companion.

At this point I would like to draw attention to the fact that pets understand us, human body language and also the spoken word, but most people cannot interpret the pets language nor perceive the meaning of their body language or posture. So, who is smarter? First we have to learn that dogs (and especially cats.) differ from the human psyche and we should by no means assume that they think and feel as we do by attributing our own, human, needs and motivations to their behaviour. They do have emotions, but they are certainly different from ours. They are rooted in the moment; animals show immediate reaction to what is happening right at that particular moment. This could be a lesson for us, being in the moment.

Dogs are pack animals

It is essential to a healthy human - dog relationship that we prove ourselves to be a strong leader, we have to learn to be a top dog that can be trusted, provides well and leads the pack. If a dog cannot find a strong leader in a person, he will try to take over, which we often label as bad behaviour. Dogs thrive when they know their place in the family, which obviously replaces the pack, the family they would have in the wild. If we, as carers make sure to fulfil the physical and psychological needs of the animal, all is well. This includes taking control at all times, especially having clear and consistent boundaries without intimidating the dog. Behavioural problems in dogs are a sign that they are suffering psychologically. I would like to stress the fact that it should be a priority for anyone to understand what caused the behaviour, and to know what can be done to address it. This could be environmental, social or, in some cases even a lack of nutrients needed to keep the body and the mind healthy - remember the micro biome affecting our brain function.

The two most prominent types of so-called bad behaviour are anxiety and aggression. These make up the greatest number of dogs taken to behavioural clinics. I read in one study that about 40% of dogs (and surprisingly also cats), have been labelled with behavioural problems, this figure being much higher in some western countries. We usually call it dog behavioural problems and put the blame on the dog, but is it really the animal? The labels of good and bad were created by humans, as is shame, which often is transferred to the pet. It may be that the dog is having a hard time adapting to the demands of humans and their social environment. I am thinking of certain breeds of working dogs kept in a small backyard with nothing to do, then getting chastised for digging or barking or even trying to escape. Others are chained up most of the time or left alone all day in the house, particularly the small breeds, suffering from separation anxiety. So, who is to blame?

There are NO 'bad' animals.

These dogs often develop behavioural issues because of too much time alone (remember they are pack animals.) and lack adequate mental and social stimulation. This leads to emotional and psychological deterioration in dogs and in a downward spiral, it weakens the human-dog bond. The reaction to this by owners is often abandoning and in worst case scenario, euthanizing a pet. Not only dogs and cats suffer from loneliness, birds, especially parrots and guinea pigs normally live in either groups or pairs; like the parrots who partner for life. Learning to recognize what triggers specific behaviours and developing a safer, more effective strategy for overcoming them is vital. Living with a companion animal is not so different from living in a human relationship. It can be wonderful, loving and nourishing for both sides, but also emotionally complex and stressful. What is distressing to a human can be just as distressing to the pet and very often we can link the quality of life of people to the quality of the pet's life. It is immensely rewarding to recognise the differences in species, at the same time realizing we all want food, water, comfort, companionship and safety.

They 'see' the world through their noses.

Humans and dogs experience the world through a very different combination of senses. To most humans, *sight* is the most important sense, followed by *touch, sound,* and *smell*. For dogs, the order is *smell, sight, sound,* and then *touch*, with a dog's sense of smell being by far the most important and so much stronger than humans. This teaches us to take care of their needs in that order. For many years, specific breeds of dogs have rescued people buried in the snow or from under rubble after earthquakes, even tracking down someone who is lost. We are familiar with dogs at the airport sniffing out drugs and other things they have been taught to find; and amazingly they can smell even one single termite when trained. Some can even smell cancer, as I have read some years ago.

Therapy dogs are well known for providing loving affection and comfort to the elderly in retirement and nursing homes, bringing joy to people in hospitals, as well as to mental institutions and prisons. Dogs as companions are also helping physically or mentally challenged children and adults to lead a happier life. There are even therapy horses, calming stressed managers and other individuals in weekend workshops. There are specific sessions with horses for women in abusive relationships, riding for the disabled, and I have also heard of horses visiting the terminal ill in hospitals. Do they feel empathy, do they realize our pain? What do they know about us that we can't fix ourselves? Horses are exceptionally sensitive animals, is it this sensitivity that detects human problems?

Despite all that animals do for us, they are still used for profit, abused, cruelly treated, slaughtered in the most horrible way, and sometimes driven to extinction. So, why do we love our pets so much? Is there also a touch of guilt about what we do to the rest of the animal kingdom? Is it ok to abuse one species and adore another? It's not immediately obvious why humans should bond so closely with another species, our hunting days are over. Is it because we instinctively know they are honest and loyal? They cannot lie or hide their feelings as our fellow humans might sometimes do. I think in this context we are unique, I believe we search for a bond, a connection to something that is greater than us and the dogs, cats, horses, birds and other animals that have graciously accepted the task to fulfil our needs.

At times, we feel good when another being is dependent on us, and we obtain psychological comfort and a certain satisfaction from being perceived positively by another, in this case a pet. Their love is unconditional, and they continue to love us regardless of any personal flaws that might cause other people to stop loving us. In human relationships, love is often conditional, with the possible exception of a parent's love for their children. The bond humans have with pets might trigger the protective and nurturing instincts; companionship is more likely for single people or seniors. Dogs have been bred for hunting, herding or guarding for many years, but nowadays cats and especially dogs are designed for physical appearances to appeal to our eyes, for coats that shed less hair and maybe also to fulfil the subconscious picture of ourselves, to satisfy our ego.

As mentioned previously, the fact that we treat our pets as infants throughout their lives, might have much to do with the emotions we are seeking. Like people favouring more small and cuddly breeds, not only because of a smaller living spaces, but also to satisfy the need for nurturing in a world where it is getting more difficult to find a caring partner; a world that can be inhuman and cruel. Most probably our love for them has multiple factors, not least is the fact that we have deliberately bred the physical characteristics into our pets to make them more appealing to us. In nature, different animal species sometimes form a social bond; not only as symbiotic relationships where they help each other to hunt for food, protect each other from predators, or clean each other from parasites, but also exhibiting empathy for another. There are many studies by naturalists of amazing cooperation between species and to our astonishment we learn how intricate the lives of animals are, never mind if it is a fish, an insect or mammal.

So much can be learned from nature and its inhabitants.

Chapter Three

The spiritual part of life

"There is a field out there beyond right doing or wrongdoing, I'll meet you there." Rumi

It is said that we are spirits in human form and when we die, we just remove our spacesuit and become spirits again. Did we come here to learn? To experience? Bruce Lipton, the famous biologist whom we have to thank for his work on *Epigenetics*, said once if we didn't come to live on this planet, we wouldn't know how chocolate tastes. This is said with tongue in cheek but who knows, it may be about experience. Unfortunately, we often divide our experiences into good and bad, which is a human trait – we often end up feeling shame or regret. I believe that learning through experience is what is important, with the emphasis on learning.

So, I have to ask: why is it humans that have to learn, not all other organisms on earth? Why shouldn't our pets not be on a learning curve like us? Or are they, and we can learn from each other? They are certainly part of creation and have spirit and soul like all animals and who can prove that plants aren't having a spiritual experience?? With the growing realisation that we are all made from the same building blocks of life, we could all be linked physically, mentally and spiritually.

Is there a spirit realm? Having had the experience of being contacted by deceased persons myself, I believe there is. We have the ancient wisdom, legends and myths telling us about the spirit world, which come from a seed of truth. There are intuitive people getting in contact with people that have crossed over, most of us have heard about it and wondered. A universal consciousness pervades and connects everything, planets, plants, animals, so called inanimate matter, and humans in subtle and unseen ways. There is a telepathic connection available to us called 'Interspecies Communication', which could link us directly to the spirit in all beings. It is based on the recognition that all beings on this earth are intelligent in their own way and connected to the creator. So, it follows that we all can inter-relate and communicate. We are able to experience this as direct thought transmission, images, feelings and concepts from other species and when mutual understanding occurs, fear and aggression are replaced by mutual respect and trust.

When we connect as spirits and share each other's unique expression of life, there is no need for categories of separation, or even a cause for alienation. Celebrating the differences and enjoying the feeling of oneness of our essential nature opens the door for learning, sharing this wonderful planet and living in harmony. When people divorce themselves from nature, from the spiritual essence that flows through all of life, and only pursue material goods and personal power, their relationship with their fellow creatures often assumes the shallow character of owner and possession. Just look at the cruelty towards other living beings all over the world. Without the spiritual connection, even when they profess love for their pets, some people may expect the animals to supply the emotional and spiritual sustenance that they are lacking within themselves.

Spirit is everywhere!

How different the relationships are when our animal friends are viewed and accepted as equal fellow spiritual beings. Beings allowed to express their own dignity, while enjoying companionship with us; and us with them. As individuals, animals in their physical nature, and with their mental and spiritual qualities, they can express themselves in their unique way. Like us, they may have a specific purpose in the universe. It is good to study biology and psychology and learn about particular needs and behaviour, but this will not teach us everything about a species. We can't separate the physical body from the spiritual aspect of a living being.
I see animals, plants, rocks and other non-human forms as the spiritual guardians or keepers on the planet. They never lose their awareness of

themselves as spirit and their innate connection to all of life. They seem to be intertwined with the earth. Humans, as late comers on this planet, appear to need the most education to master their existence. Unlike most animals, we struggle with the complexity of life and very often feel separate from the whole, and have problems acknowledging ourselves as spiritual beings. This sometimes leaves us feeling alienated in the material world.

Native cultures tell us that we, living in the western countries and spreading havoc in our environment, have separated from spirit, alienated ourselves from source. This explains the destruction we see everywhere on the planet. Ancient, and even modern tribal cultures recognize the connection to all life through ceremonial rituals such as observance of the seasons. They acknowledge animals and plants, indeed all of creation, as being part of themselves, and necessary for their physical, mental and spiritual wellbeing. In some cultures, people go on a quest to find their spirit animals which come to them in visions or dreams, or perhaps during a fast. An animal spirit is the spiritual energy of the animal on earth. The animal spirit is greater than the actual animal because it embodies the essence of that animal spirit itself. It has a special meaning to the person and will act as a guardian and teacher. Native spiritual leaders and healers, the shamans, are believed to have spiritual connections with animals and all elements of nature.

Shamanism has had a renaissance in recent years, and I think it appeals to many of us just because of the spiritual aspect of it. We intuitively know there is a part of us missing, and we search for a connection. Subconsciously, we want to awaken to our true essence and enjoy clarity and a sense of purpose. It might free us from our past, bring balance to our life, and heal physical ailments. We, who are separated from existence through logic, scientific analysis and rationality, do need to re-connect to the animals, plants and the earth. Humans need the animals and all other life forms on many levels, from biological to spiritual.

Why not learn from the spirit of the pet in your care?

Not only can we use telepathy to connect, there is another tool available to us called intuition. We all have it, and it works. Intuition does not rely on previous knowledge; it works hand in hand with imagination and inspiration and leads us to see a different perspective. It supports us in our survival and provides us with the best outcome in life -- if we listen to it!

Intuition is a normal human function; we all have it.

Intuition doesn't need any studies or research. As a matter of fact, many scientists work with their intuition. The best example is Albert Einstein, whose scientific inspirations came to him in a dream. Our intuition is always ready to guide us to the actions that will make the most of a situation. It ensures our evolutionary potential and this knowledge seems to be present in all cells (or maybe in all atoms.), a multi-dimensional guidance system. If this spiritual connection is present in all cells of our body, then it could connect us with everything there is, on a level we don't fully understand as yet. But not knowing how it works should not stop us from graciously accepting it. It is understandable that many people are somewhat frightened when experiencing the inner guidance system for the first time, we have been conditioned to only believe what we can touch, see or a so called authority telling us this is reality. Even science has mostly theories which, down the track, are superseded by new ones. There is so much to be discovered.

We simply need to remember our gift of intuition, which serves both our material and our spiritual aspects of who we are as human beings. We certainly could develop our skills by listening to our pets and train ourselves to be competent in intuiting the need of others. This intuition could help us with sick, old and dying animals, asking them if the time has come. Unfortunately, pets do not live as long as humans, so it is always sad to part with them. They leave their body, as we will one day, but we can get in touch with their spirit. It seems they are quite at ease when the end comes which is only a transition into the spirit world anyway. It is said we exist in spirit until the time comes to take on earthly forms again. Our spirit energy must live on according to the laws of physics which are the laws of the cosmos.

Energy can be transferred to other objects or converted into different forms, but cannot be created or destroyed.

Can we get in touch with departed pets? Wouldn't that be wonderful and comforting? Many people believe so and many have experienced it. Afterlife communication with pets can help the grieving process and ease our loss. Our pet's love is purely unconditional. They just want to be loved and to share their love. I am positive this continues into the afterlife and is communicated to their partner here on earth through several different means and different types of senses. Spirit vibrates with a higher energy so their presence might feel like goose bumps, a chill, static electricity or hairs standing up on end which happens to me in times like that. Others report they smell their departed animal friend, feel something is jumping on the bed, they might hear little feet running through the house, or feel a presence sitting next to them on the couch.

We might have no control over this process, but I believe once connected through love in life we will always be connected in spirit as well. Being still and in a meditative state opens us up to receive signs, emotions like sadness, upset or grieving might hinder this connection. All the more important to practice meditation. Getting in touch spiritually with our companions, not only helps to overcome our grief, but we also know that they are okay and will wait for us when it is our time to join them in the afterlife. Whether or not you receive a sign or message from an animal you love, you can rest assured that anyone who is connected to you through love and spirit will always stay connected to you. Love never dies.

Crackle the "Centre of the known Universe"

Chapter Four

The connection to all there is

The Real World Wide Web

When breaking up all matter, may it be human, animal, plant, earth or a star we find the smallest amount of matter called an atom. We learned in school about the periodic table telling us about the elements of which everything is made of. Atoms are the smallest particle that retains its identity as a chemical element; it consists of a nucleus surrounded by electrons. The nucleus, which is the centre, contains many smaller bits until we encounter the electrons. These are like a field or a wave, as opposed to the idea in the early 1900's of balls moving around the centre. For our understanding here, it is only necessary to realize that all matter is made up of these atoms bonding together to build molecules. These combine into compounds, then organs, bodies, plants, everything on earth and the cosmos and form the basis of all we know. At this point in time we can only guess at the underlying forces or intelligent information contained within all matter, indeed throughout the universe.

We are all made from star stuff!

The world is not a fragmented and mechanical place as we have been told for the last few hundred years; and how it is still taught in some schools. It is a holistic world where are all things are connected, never mind the distance. *Quantum entanglement* describes the phenomenon where two particles which interact with each other can remain connected, instantaneously sharing their physical states no matter how far apart they are. From the viewpoint of quantum physics, the observer and the phenomenon are inseparably linked.

So, from here on you, the reader, and I are also linked.

The lives on this planet are so intertwined with all there is, we cannot stand alone. We fall and stand with our fellow beings, and with this, I mean all life forms on earth. This time in history, more than ever before, we need to develop more understanding and common sense towards our companions, indeed towards all beings. It is very humbling to realize, not one single animal or plant needs us for their survival, but humans could not survive at all without them.

All organisms are biological, intelligent computers, able to transmit and receive. We, as humans, are like a radio antenna that picks up thoughts not only from our immediate surroundings but also from a distance as *quantum theory* elegantly explains - all is connected through space and time. So, if we are functioning similar to an antenna, we are also able to transmit. In my view, telepathy is a part of this, and most of us have experienced this at some stage of our lives. It could be the message we get from a loved person far away or even 'knowing' a loved one has died. Could intuitive hunches contain information about future events? Is it possible to perceive messages and information without the use of the ordinary senses?

Earth's magnetic field is a carrier of biologically relevant information that connects all living beings. All of us affect the global information field with our thoughts, feelings and emotions, not the least with our artificial world wide web feeding all kinds of junk into the ether. Therefore, it is of the utmost importance to take great care of our output and energy and what we feed into the field every second. While many of the mainstream scientists still call anything connected with intuition nonsense, an increasing number of independent and more enlightened researchers, scientists and lay people are taking such phenomena seriously and eventually science will have to accommodate those experiences we call psychic and magic. Not so very long ago a mobile phone would have been considered magic.

Remote viewing has been around since the early 1900's It was first used by the military to spy on their perceived enemy, (and probably still is). It is a method now taught in many countries, and available for everyone who is interested. Remote viewing means that we can 'tune' into other places and people, past, present and future, no matter where they are located. In the training we learn to distinguish between imagination and true intuitive perception. Having read many articles and books about remote viewing, one astounding fact really stuck in my mind, one remote viewer said that the people he observed actually noticed he was 'viewing' them. Somehow the connection was felt. These days, Remote Viewing is taught to businesspeople, corporations, archaeologists, police, and medical doctors, just to name a few. I believe we all have this ability to tune into the world around us, into time and space.

We know about *Medical Intuitives*, being sensitive people with insight into physical and emotional ailments of their clients. They are able to point out blockages, and discover damaging patterns in life, therefore, presenting an opportunity for the patient to let go of struggle and self-sabotage. Our body holds vibrational patterns, messages from the past or present, and these messages can be read by a Medical Intuitive to help identify the root cause of the discomfort.

As Einstein said: "Spooky Action at a Distance."

Could entangled minds result in the experience of hearing the telephone ring and instantly know who is on the other end? Haven't we all had experiences like that? Could this also work with animals? I firmly believe so and, in my life, I have experienced this with animals, plants and the occasional human.

The book 'Dogs that know when their owners come home', written by biologist Rupert Sheldrake some years ago, explains about the telepathic connection animals have with their people, especially dogs and cats. I recommend reading it. He documented many cases that showed dogs and cats anticipating the return of their owners by waiting at a door or window even when arriving at random times, or in a taxi instead of in their own car. They anticipate their people going on holidays (I have my own experience to vouch for that), of being fed, cats disappearing when their owners intend to take them to the vet, dogs knowing when going for a walk, even when it is only a thought in the mind of the person. On his website he invites people to take part and contribute to his research.

The relationship we share with our pets goes beyond just giving commands or taking them for walks, there are moments when a single gaze is enough to communicate in an unspoken, universal language. When the bond with an animal is strong, sometimes even the thought of a command is enough for the animal to respond to it. This is true, I experienced this with my dog Lotti, just a look and a thought and she complied. A great example was my featherless cockatoo, Crackle, rescued from a farm where he could only forage on the ground. He was found with a broken wing and could never fly. Unfortunately, nobody there took any care offering him cockatoo 'food'. So, he could only eat what he found on the ground. Because of a lack of proper nutrition, he subsequently lost all his feathers, except one of the crest feathers which he raised when excited. It was a funny sight to see.

When the time came to cut his beak I had to hide my thoughts, and the clippers of course, otherwise he would pick up on the pictures in my head and disappear or when in his cage get stressed. I used to sing to cover my intention so he could not read my mind. Then I would grab him unexpectedly, gently of course, and proceeded to cut his beak. Even the cat that accompanied me in my life for 19 years would follow my silent command. Of course, cats are their own 'person' so she would do this only occasionally.

> As the saying goes: "Dogs have masters, cats have servants."

Morphogenic or *Morphic Fields* is a term re-discovered by the aforementioned Biologist, *Rupert Sheldrake*. It is now accepted by forward thinking researchers and scientists. We understand that they are non-local, active information fields which all species, including humans of course, possess. These morphic fields are responsible for the development and maintenance of bodily form, social and cultural fields in plants and animals. They are a like an organizing field. Whatever the explanation of its origin, once a new morphic pattern – a new pattern of organization/idea/invention – has come into being, this field becomes stronger through repetition.

The same pattern becomes more likely to happen again, even with a physical distance. The more often patterns are repeated in a species, the more probable it becomes for others to follow suit. The fields contain a kind of cumulative memory and eventually evolve in time and form the basis of habits. When some or many information fields, for whatever reason, become coherent and resonant, they interact and create a new, highly structured information field accessible by others at any distance.

This explains the hundredth monkey principle.

So far no one claims to understand how this works or where these fields are, but to dismiss something because we do not have an explanation for it, is not a good scientific approach. Most likely we are enveloped in them, a bit like swimming in a sea of information. My own experience confirms this. While visiting monasteries in remote mountainous places in China, and training with the monks there, I felt like the air was thick and I could 'draw' information/knowledge out of it. It was an amazing state to be in. So, it makes sense to say we live in a holistic ecology which views all living beings and its environment as a single system. It is a holistic world where are all things are connected.

Biophilia - connection to nature.

Everything we do to the ecosystem of the earth we do to ourselves. Not only modern pollution and toxins make us ill; so does our disconnection from nature. I believe that the human quest for meaning only finds answers when we look at our roots, our origins. Is it this deeper contact with nature that lets us 'converse' with other species? Looking at the number of books on the market concerning communication with animals, we are coming closer to the idea that it is not just childish imagination and projection. I believe by using our intuition and telepathy we are able to enter into the holistic realm, and also touch on the morphic fields of other species. We simply need to remember our gift of intuition; some call it a hunch. We often hear of successful people acting on a hunch or calling it a gut feeling, it seems it doesn't involve the brain, what a relief. We certainly could train and develop our skills by 'intuiting' our pets and even plants in the home. They will be happy that you heard them, took notice of them and you will always get an answer.

> *It boils down to knowing without knowing how you knew.*

I am sure everyone has heard of, or perhaps even experienced hugging a tree when stressed. Not only do they contribute to the environment by providing oxygen as a result of photosynthesis, conserving water, preserving soil and supporting wildlife, but they also energize us humans. Trees are intelligent and nurturing and have a sense of touch and share their energy with us when we ask humbly and approach them in a receptive manner. Trees have the power to unlock our intuition, help us on our spiritual journey and sometimes even graciously offer answers to our earthly problems. Maybe they can look into our soul. We should always ask for permission first, and afterwards give thanks for their help. Sitting quietly, not expecting anything, and opening our hearts and minds to receive helps to create the connection. Whatever is entering the mind is fine; just letting go of stressful thoughts and feelings is okay as well.

The *World Tree* motif is known to all of us, sometimes referred to as the *Tree of Life*, depicting the connection of cosmos and earth. The roots are anchored in the earth, the branches reaching to heaven; aren't we as humans similar? This theme can be found in the mythologies of ancient cultures all over the world. Some hold sacred a local tree species, like the oak in Celtic traditions, the cedars of Lebanon or even the redwoods in California. Indeed, we are just re-discovering the connections we have with all plants and animals as soon as we release our spirit to freely meld with others.

There are therapies now offered for traumatized people such as war veterans, which involves simply being in a forest to help resolve their stress. It really seems crazy to me that we make a science out of something that has been a fact to humans for thousands of years. My own experience confirms this connection, I often get messages from plants asking for help. Something makes me turn around and there is a plant in need of water. On occasion, I have proven to people that plants flower for me. I want to stress the fact that it is not me that makes them do it, nor do I expect them to comply, they simply want to please me as many fellow gardeners can verify, just as our pets do. It is usually called a green thumb, but I see it as some sort of inter-relationship between humans and plants, available to, and enjoyed by anyone.

There is another interesting tale I would like to share with you. This is about a tree I planted some years ago, which grew for some months but then died down for no apparent reason, to me anyway. I stood in front of it and kept the thought of an axe in my head, lo and behold, it started to sprout new shoots within a few days. The tree and I repeated this game 3 times, but then I felt there must have been reasons not known to me, so I let it go and finally dug it out and planted something else there. Maybe these 'conversations' are based on the morphic fields discussed earlier, as plants do not have a brain or a nervous system but nevertheless 'hear' us.

A gentleman named *Clive Backster* worked for the CIA using a polygraph in the 1960's, commonly known as a lie detector, when by chance he hooked up one of the office plants to it. He was astonished how it reacted to his thoughts. A polygraph measures the electrical resistance of the skin as a result of experiencing emotional states, like being stressed, fearful or nervous. Whenever we are emotionally aroused, the electrical conductivity of our skin subtly changes; I believe it is still used by the police. Eventually he did many more tests with plants, bacteria (yoghurt.) and even human cells and spent the rest of his long life in his institute, studying the ability of plants to communicate with the environment. It is a long story and available on the internet as well as in books.

There are institutes around the world researching plant behaviour, emotions and the interaction with their environment. An Italian Neurobiologist and author, *Stefano Mancuso*, says that plants are as sophisticated in behaviour as animals, but their potential has not been recognized because they operate on a time scale which is much less than the animals, everything happens slower. They are dynamic and sensitive organisms and have a recognition of self and non self. They communicate with each other, fighting over resources but also, and please everyone take note: they help each other as well. Mainstream science usually explains the intelligence of plant behaviour in terms of electrical and chemical responses without leaving the discussion open to the possibility that thoughts are not stored in the brain but in a universal information field.

A few years ago, I bought a gadget which is hooked up to a leaf on a plant, and when switched on, the electrical impulses of the plant are turned into musical sounds. Every one of the plants tested sings in its own rhythm, in a different pitch; some happily babbling, and others in a rather slow and timid way. This shows again, one does not need a brain or a nervous system to converse and connect with our fellow earthly organisms. This would confirm the experience I had of information/knowledge available to me from the air when visiting China. This strong feeling at a temple high up in the mountains, convinced me that we can absorb information through the skin, not only through our sensory organs.

Deep inside, we know something is missing and we yearn for this 'something'. Not only a peaceful, kinder, and simpler way of living but also a meaningful connection to everything. The human cost of alienating from nature can be seen in the stressed and depressed population with higher rates of physical illness. We feel disconnected, overwhelmed and unsupported in the way we have organised our so-called modern lives. Wars, killing and cruelty seem to be a human trait; it has been going on for thousands of years. No other species is so hell bent on devastating their own living space, while a minority tries to save, recover, and clean up what the mainstream messed up.

We desperately have to re-think our way of living!

Subconsciously, we know that all the destructive ways employed in western society in the last 200 years will impact all lives, and eventually destroy everything, not only us. It is sad to know that we are sabotaging the very life force we call nature. On a positive note, nature does not give up, sometimes we feel her presence and the invitation to come closer. Everything around us is alive and conscious in its own particular way. We can start to connect with our pets and house plants; then progress to the garden and the nature spirits. I talk to my car and laptop, thanking them for their service. Showing gratitude alters our energetic field and influences everything. Remember we all made from similar materials. If we perceive animals and plants as sentient beings rather than a resource, it might help us to find new and harmonious ways of living and help us humans to live a better life.

One big hurdle to overcome is our expectations; this can block the connection. We can then become disappointed, and sometimes give up. We have been trained to get instant answers these days, so remember to give it time. Be willing and open minded, respectful and humble, and most of all be playful. Children are so much more open to invisible spirits and see it as fun - until school gets hold of them and teaches them 'real life'. Slowly, mainstream science is arriving at a radically different understanding. While the body appears to be material, it is really a field of energy and intelligence that is inextricably connected to the cosmic mind. All thoughts, perceptions, memories, emotions, and feelings in our mind influence every cell of our body. When we have a loving thought or focus on a happy memory or feeling, our brain triggers a cascade of molecules that promote wellbeing in our physiology. The energy body serves as the template for the physical body. When the energy body is balanced and clear, the physical body is healthy. On the other hand, when the energy body is out of balance and congested, it filters into the physical body and symptoms develop.

Daoist teachings say: "Where thought goes, energy follows."

Opening up to and connecting to natures extraordinary intelligence and eventually learning to connect on a deeper level, helps us to understand the innate nature of animals, specifically our pets. We would do well to remember that the same water that flows in the ocean, runs through our bloodstream; and the same vitamins and minerals in nature are the very substance from which our bones and body are built.

Mark Twain sure had it right when he said, "If man could be crossed with a cat it would improve man, but it would deteriorate the cat."

Chapter Five

Species appropriate diet

Let food be thy medicine and medicine thy food

Hippocrates knew what could heal and keep us healthy. It must be obvious to most people that we strayed from that path years ago; and despite an enormous amount of information out in the public arena, it seems to get worse. From my point of view, health starts at home, especially these days, it boils down to making informed choices daily. One doesn't have to study rocket science to realize (or to remind oneself) that only what comes from nature, fresh and unadulterated, is of value to us as living beings.

Anything that has been processed in a factory should be avoided despite claims made by the manufacturer. No one can convince me that any food is improved by technology or foreign chemicals. These foods, I love the expression Franken foods, are not even good for the compost. Eating manufactured foods devoid of life and valuable natural compounds like vitamins, minerals, phytonutrients, or enzymes, just to name a few, results in deficiencies and eventually leading to symptoms and further deterioration and an unhappy life.

Today's pets suffer from very similar diseases to people. The right diet is the bricks and mortar in health. Putting a little thought into what you feed your cat or dog pays big dividends over a lifetime. It quite possibly helps them to avoid serious and costly illnesses. Apart from the cost involved, it is our duty to the animals to feed what is right and healthy for that species.

Dead foods - sick bodies!

I see many pets, including horses and other domestic animals, as prisoners; confined to places in our human world, and given foods that are certainly not always what they need. They are not able to forage for the grasses, herbs, or even minerals which they instinctively seek out in nature to gain balance in their health. In their natural habitat, animals look for what they lack and walk many miles to seek out salt deposits, certain kind of mineral or specific grasses, leaves or seeds that provides them with the nutrients for healing.

In the wild, the canine species eats the whole animal, getting a selection of nutrients from muscle and organ meat, bones, cartilage and stomach contents, even fur, feathers and feet in the case of birds. The complexity and the inherent knowledge of a species of what they need to stay healthy is astounding. If an organism is not interfered with in any way and given what it needs, it shows an innate wisdom of organisation, meaning health and wellbeing is more likely. This not only applies to animals; we also have this inbuilt wisdom - we just don't act on it very often. Sadly, health is one of those things we only appreciate when it is failing. Observing the natural laws gives us a chance to keep our bodies in good shape, or provides the support needed to get back to health. This goes for a human and an animal body alike.

The simplicity lies in nature's request to observe those laws and to acknowledge the rules of the game. It is not necessary to understand everything in detail. Let's face it science does not really know what life is and how it came to thrive, how some species became extinct, others emerged and multiplied to inhabit this planet. Trillions of cells make up our bodies, a few less for a cricket, a few more for a human or an elephant; all want to be fed and nature provides for all of us.

We distinguish between **Macronutrients** *and* **Micronutrients.**

Macronutrients are **proteins, fats** and **carbohydrates**; everybody is familiar with these. Meat of course, is the most well know **protein** supply, but there are proteins contained in many plants and vegetarians can do well eating a varied diet. For most of us there is no need to have animal protein, this can be gained from other sources. For me personally ethics play the main role in not eating meat. In my view it is the cruelty in keeping animals the way we do, like it is only a commodity instead of a living, feeling organism. I am talking about large scale breeding of livestock, not of the small farmer who is concerned about the health and wellbeing of his animals. This was the practice many years ago before the greediness of our so-called modern society took over, and people are less concerned where food, especially meat is coming from.

Fats are necessary for all mammals. Not only does the brain consist of fatty tissue (about 60%), but good fats and oils in a human diet are essential for many other important functions in the body. When I say good fats, I mean those coming from a natural source; not the adulterated stuff the factories churn out and sell in clear plastic bottles. For many years people were warned not to eat fats. As a result, they banished it from their diet as much as possible and the slogan 'fat-free or low-fat' was everywhere. Unfortunately, it still lingers on. Consumers, please realize the fact that the low-fat products have been altered in their composition and the fat content removed. Fat carries taste so it has to be replaced by other fillers, like sugar, salt or flavour enhancers (MSG) to offer a tasty product that people will buy. Reason enough not to eat the fat free products. The fact is, we all need good, fresh fats daily.

What makes a fat or oil different from another, is the length and shape of the carbon chain, and the number of hydrogen atoms connected to the carbon atoms. Seemingly slight differences in structure, translate into crucial differences in form and function. Then we have simple and complex **carbohydrates**. The simple ones are refined sugars like in fruit (fructose), milk (lactose) and refined sugar (sucrose). The complex carbohydrates which include all kinds of whole grains, rice, potatoes, beans, lentils etc. are digested more slowly. This makes them better for the human digestive system because of the fiber it contains. This means a product should not be refined to remove much of the fiber, for example stripping the husk of wheat to bake bread with the de-natured white flour. Nature made it for eating whole. For canines, this is another story altogether.

Micronutrients are **vitamins** and **minerals** which are also necessary for life. All organisms need *micronutrients*, just in a smaller quantity than the *macronutrients*. Some of them are needed only in a tiny amount, this is the reason why they are labeled Micro, nevertheless they are just as important. **Vitamins** are organic compounds made by plants and animals which can be broken down by heat, acid or air. **Minerals** found in most soils are inorganic and cannot be useful for our digestive system. They are only available for humans after the plants have digested them. Then there are trace elements like boron, selenium, chromium, copper and many more, needed in even smaller quantities but nevertheless just as essential as vitamins and minerals.

There are deposits of ancient plant matter called *Shilajit*. These are found primarily in the Himalayas and in the mountainous regions of Russia. Over millions of years, this plant matter has been broken down and decomposed by natural processes to form large organic deposits. Water seeps through these deposits collecting many minerals, organic acids and other beneficial nutrients; and eventually accumulates in rocks and crevices. *Shilajit,* a black tar like mass, is rich in amino acids and mineral complexes. It contains more than 85 vital minerals in bio-active form to promote vitality, strength and endurance in humans and pets alike. This *Shilajit* is the natural source of *fulvic acid* used often by gardeners. They know how vital this compound is for plants to grow strong and healthy. The *fulvic acid* activates the nutrients within the soil (enzymes), so that they can be utilised by the plants. This is similar to the enzymes helping to digest food in the human body.

> *Everything in nature is designed to keep all life balanced.*

When we eat, we consume the vitamins plants and animals manufactured in their bodies and the minerals they absorbed. An adequate intake of all micronutrients is necessary for optimal health. Each vitamin and mineral or trace element has a specific role in our body, and they all work in synergy. Not only are they essential for building healthy bodies but also, specifically in our time, play a role in preventing and fighting disease. Fortunately, vitamins and minerals bind some of the toxins we ingest and move them out of the body. The nutrient content of each food is different, so naturally it's best to eat a variety of foods to get enough vitamins and minerals. Depending on the soil they are grown in and how they are treated and stored makes a huge difference.

It wasn't that long ago that the word 'organic' became popular, like it was something newly invented. 30-40 years ago, it was normal to grow vegetable in the backyard without artificial additives and people pulled out or chipped the so-called weeds instead of spraying them with poisons. Natural enzymes which help us to digest are found only within fresh foods and deteriorate quickly, like the vitamins, when vegetables and fruits are cooked or stored for any length of time.

Organically grown is always best, without pesticides or herbicides.

For anyone interested, there are many health sites explaining the role and function of micro- and macronutrients in detail. For instance, there are water soluble vitamins, fat soluble vitamins, macro minerals and trace minerals, all crucial for our health and wellbeing. Looking at wolves, dingoes, and other wild dogs in their natural habitat, we realize they are carnivores and their food is raw meat, bones, organ meat and some of the fur or feathers. As we learned earlier, they also eat the content of their preys' intestines which provides them with friendly bacteria. Meat eating animals mainly eat herbivores (grass eaters) but will also eat omnivores (meat and grass eaters). They seldom eat other carnivores. The stomach and intestinal content of herbivore prey contains their fermented meals and provides bacteria for digestion. I do not think it is accidental that carnivores mainly hunt herbivores. It makes sense regarding the availability of fermented plant material available in the prey.

Nature has worked it out perfectly.

Let us have a look at raw materials of life. **Macronutrients – Proteins.** Not all proteins are created equal. Proteins derived from animal tissues have a complete amino acid profile. Plant-based proteins, on the other hand, do not contain the full profile of the critical amino acids required by carnivores. Proteins consist of amino acid compounds which are the building blocks of the protein, divided into essential and non-essential ones. The essential amino acids have to be ingested with the foods, non-essential ones can be synthesized in the body

Carnivores need animal-based proteins.

The canine family requires 22 different amino acids for their very survival. Some can be synthesized in the body, but some cannot. They have to be supplied from animal protein; they are the essential amino acids necessary for their species. Proteins provide basic building blocks for tissues like muscles, hair, nails, tendons, cartilage and are responsible for transport, regulation and growth in mammals. They are essential not only for good tissue and muscle health, but also for a strong immune system and healthy hair and skin. Proteins are an important element of cells as well as providing an energy depot. The body uses protein to make enzymes, hormones and other important compounds. In comparison to fats they are used up more quickly.

As we seen above, amino acids are critical for life. **Taurine** is an amino acid found primarily in muscle meat and organs like heart, kidney and liver as well as in seafood and shellfish. Only small amounts are in dairy products, including eggs. Plants contain hardly any taurine. I feel it is important to put emphasis on the fact that the lack of taurine is a well-known nutritional problem in cats, especially if they are fed an artificial diet. It affects their health, specifically the eyes and can predispose an animal to heart failure. Dogs don't seem to suffer from it as much. As mentioned above the quality and composition of a protein is especially critical for cats, they cannot live on vegetable matter, the reason being that they lack certain enzymes to utilize plant material.

*I cannot stress enough that cats **need** fresh meat!*

Humans make their own taurine and usually live very well on plant-based protein. Even dogs as carnivores can tolerate some vegetable matter and get away with it. Canines are scavengers eating dead animals, even decomposing meat poses no problem due to the very strong hydrochloric acid killing any bacteria.

Fats
There are animal and plant-based fats. The plant-based fats have more unsaturated fatty acids than animal fats. These are divided into simple lipids, complex lipids and derived lipids. Fats are important for the transport of nutrients, protecting organs, building hormones, the nervous system and supplying energy. Fat soluble vitamins are A, D, E and K can be stored in the liver and fatty tissue until needed. I guess we all know that fats can deposit easily in tissues. They form a sort of energy reservoir there, used by the organism when the need arises, like a shortage of food. The body has its plan B when needed, but these days, it is rare for us to go hungry. This means overeating, particularly on bad fats, ends up stored in the liver and tissues. In comparison to other energy supplies, the fat stores are used slowly. High quality fats are ideal for a long term, economical energy supply, providing they are in a good balance to proteins and carbohydrates.

Earlier we learned that a body is made up of trillions of cells, forming organs, tissues, bone, hair, nails and of course the brain, building blocks for all life. Cells are a complete organism in itself with a centre which is organised into specialised compartments, a cell wall to keep the shape and an outer protective skin. This skin is called a membrane and is of utmost importance for good health in humans and animals; protecting, nourishing and being very selective in what is entering the cell. Unhealthy membranes can make the cell less efficient, affecting organs, really, the whole body. Cell membranes are vitally important because they separate the cells in the body from their outside world, similar to the function of the skin for the body as a whole.

The cell membranes are made of fatty acids and proteins and are selectively permeable, they regulate not only what enters the cell but also how much. They are like gatekeepers and we realize now what an important role they play. Interestingly cholesterol is another part of the structure of cell membranes and is not the 'baddie' it is made out to be, it is critical to health. Fats are also necessary for nerve cells, specifically in the brain and in the spinal cord, which is called the Central Nervous System. Those nerve cells have long fibres called axons, which conduct electrical impulses. To let electricity pass efficiently through the axons, an 'insulation' made up of a fatty substance called myelin, covers those fibres which appear as the white fatty matter in the brain. If this fatty sheath protecting the nerve fibres is damaged, leaving the nerves unprotected, messages can be delayed, distorted or cannot get through at all. This situation can give rise to neurological disorders. It is similar to a short circuit when the insulation on electrical wiring melts and exposes the wires.

Good nutrition is the best way to guarantee health for humans and animals. Choosing the right fats of high quality, freshness and, in the right balance, will ensure better eye and heart health. Increased brain function helps with inflammation and generally fewer health problems in our lifetime. Taking into account all of the above, we see how important fats are to mammals for growth and energy. Therefore, it is essential to make better and informed choices about what kind of fats to use and avoid hydrogenated and processed oils and fats. It makes sense feeding puppies healthy fats in the right balance, helping them to develop better brains, resulting in better behaviour. Puppies learn faster and have an improved attention span and it helps the older dogs to stay mentally sharp. It goes without saying, good healthy fats are just as important for human children to grow into smart adults, developing a strong body and mind and later in life, to help us to age better.

Fats need to be high quality and absolutely fresh. They turn rancid quickly, creating what is called free radicals which may cause harm when eaten on a regular basis. One can recognize good oils because they come in dark glass bottles, even better, buy only organic. Oils in clear plastic bottles should be avoided; not only because light will oxidize the oil over time, but also chemicals from the plastic leach into the content. One hears the importance of Omega 3-6-9 oils; all have health benefits of course and are important dietary fats. However, it is essential to get the right balance. Omega 3's are contained in mostly in fish, the 6 and 9 are in vegetable oils, nuts and seeds.

Carbohydrates
Over the last 20 years or so, carbohydrates have been rather controversial in human nutrition. One of the primary functions of carbohydrates is to provide the body with energy. These are broken down into glucose (a sugar) before entering the bloodstream and used as a source of strength and vigour. If the glucose is not used up through physical exercise/work, it will be stored in the liver as glycogen and later as fat. Fatty livers are not necessarily caused by too much alcohol consumption as has been thought for a long time. Sugar, soft drinks, sweets, fruit juices, fried foods, pasta, white rice and bread are all carbohydrates. They can contribute to a fatty liver and should be avoided, at least eaten only occasionally. Today we even have children presenting with fatty livers as well as diabetes because of overconsumption of carbs.

The crucial factors are how much and what kind of carbohydrates we eat, if it is highly refined and processed, and also if it has been exposed to herbicides and pesticides. Processing removes some or all of the nutrients and other compounds important for health. White flour is an example of refined carbohydrates, lacking in fibre, vitamins B and E and minerals due to processing. This makes it less nutritious than unrefined flour. Of course, the length of storage could also pose a problem. Legumes, brown rice, whole grains, tubers, nuts and seeds and vegetable all are good carbohydrates for us humans. The ones to avoid are all processed grains, sugar and sugar containing food items, fruit juices, sweets etc. as mentioned above. I am positive we all know what is beneficial for the body and what is not.

Another reason I personally don't recommend eating too much wheat, especially refined, is because wheat, corn, soy and some other grains, have been hybridized in the 20th century and aren't the original plants anymore. In the last 50 years, many other compounds and genes have been introduced into the original grain to serve purposes like a shorter stem for easy harvesting, for longer storage, not being eaten by pests, and to tolerate being sprayed with herbicides. This method of introducing other genes into plants is called Genetically Modified Organisms, GMO for short. There is another reason for altering plants, the giant chemical companies own the patent for the grains and plants so profit from selling the seeds. No wonder many of us have all kinds of health issues.

Genetically altered grains and vegetables should be avoided if possible.

Since dogs are not biologically designed to eat and digest foods high in carbohydrates in the form of grains, they should be fed only a tiny amount or none at all. Carbohydrates cannot be effectively digested and tend to stay in the dog's digestive tract for a longer period of time. This can lead to gas and bowel irritations. The dog's feces will be bulky and very smelly because the fermentation is in the gut instead of a correct digestion. Of course, these problems are very similar to fermentation in the human digestive tract, usually caused by a lack of digestive enzymes, but can have other, more severe, reasons. They are called digestive enzymes because they help to process various foods, come in many different strains and live in our intestines. They are essential for the breakdown of carbohydrates, fats, proteins, lactose and plant fibers. Naturally, each species of animal would have different groups of enzymes in their gut, depending on their specific diet.

Our ancestors ate unprocessed carbohydrates, such as all kinds of grains, tubers and legumes. Some cultures, like the Asians, have planted rice for thousands of years. I'm not sure when rice was first processed, but before the industrial revolution, the whole grain (brown) rice would have been the staple diet in many Asian countries. Studies have linked carbohydrates from various grains to such health issues as allergies, arthritis, and seizures to name just a few. In addition, excessive starches in the dogs' gut can decrease the absorption of minerals, such as calcium, zinc, iron, and magnesium. I have to mention it again, cats are especially vulnerable, they have no chance of digesting any carbohydrates.

Simple carbohydrates eaten on a permanent basis, especially if they are the biggest part of the daily diet, predisposes humans as well as animals to diabetes. There are more and more dogs and cats treated for diabetes. As we discussed earlier, these turn into sugars, then enter the bloodstream. If the blood sugar content cannot be reduced by insulin, a hormone made by the pancreas, eventually diabetes results. More details on diabetes can be found on many health sites on the web.

*I want to stress the fact that **ALL** vitamins, minerals and trace elements are equally important. I have only listed a few which I feel need an explanation.*

Vitamins
Vitamins are necessary in any organism to support growth; they are responsible, together with enzymes and co-enzymes, for all the metabolic processes. They are needed to heal wounds, repair cellular damage, support the immune system, boost blood antioxidant level, help convert food into energy. Vitamins originate in plants, but our large intestine assembles some of them. There are fat-soluble vitamins like A, D, E, K, as mentioned earlier, which can be stored for a longer period and water-soluble ones like the B group and Vitamin C, needing to be replaced periodically. The water-soluble ones are contained in the moist part of foods and absorbed directly into the bloodstream as the food is broken down during digestion.

It is a bit more complicated for the fat-soluble vitamins, they need bile to be absorbed and the nutrients then get taken up through the walls of the intestines. Fatty foods and oils are a reservoir of the fat-soluble vitamins and the body stores them in the liver and fatty tissues to be released when needed. Vitamin C is an essential one, meaning it can't be produced by the human body. Therefore, we need to eat fresh vitamin rich foods daily or take a supplement. I would advise taking supplements due to so many deficient foods as well as our contaminated environment. Dogs can produce or synthesize, enough vitamin C for their own needs in normal times. When stressed or sick, their vitamin stores can get depleted quickly. As with us humans, even emotional stress (e.g. by a change in life situations) can affect the Vitamin C level in a pet.

We touched on Vitamin D in Chapter 1. I mentioned the lack of sunlight on our bodies these days; and how deficient many people have become because of our so-called modern lifestyle. Our ancestors used to be outside all day. Summer and winter and cultures living in cold northern countries eat fatty fish to compensate for the lack of sunlight to get enough vitamin D. It has only been known since the late 1800's, after children in the previous centuries, especially since the industrial revolution, were reported to have skeletal deformities, (rickets), that a lack in vitamin D was actually the problem. Of course, the health consequences of being vitamin D deficient goes far beyond rickets, today we know the significance of not getting enough of this vitamin for strong bones by regulating the calcium absorption and generally improved resistance against diseases.

I feel it is important to mention the production of synthetic vitamins and other supplements. This process is very different to the way plants and animals create them; it happens in the laboratory. Despite having the same chemical formula, your body may react differently to synthetic nutrients. Additionally, it's unclear how well synthetic nutrients are absorbed and used in the body. Some may be more easily absorbed, others not. The outer skin of cells, the membrane, has 'docking stations' so only compounds which are useful and recognized by the membrane and will be let in. Synthetic vitamins are certainly cheap to make and last much longer on the shelf than vitamins extracted from plants, profit before health.

Anything that lasts for a long time should be avoided, it is unnatural.

Whole food supplements are extracted only from ripe, whole fruits, vegetables or grains that have been carefully processed into a liquid, powder (capsules) or pressed into tablets, retaining all the goodness naturally occurring in the original plant. Synthetic supplements are isolated or simulated nutrients, made in the laboratory. They do not take into account all the many phytonutrients, co-factors and enzymes that come with whole foods or supplements made from the extracts from plants. Unfortunately, our soils around the world are getting more and more depleted; even naturally and organically grown vegetable have less nutrients these days. This has led to the inevitable need for many of us to supplement ourselves, and our pets with the appropriate vitamins and minerals from respectable companies.

Minerals

Essential minerals, like Calcium, Chloride, Magnesium, Potassium, Phosphorus, Silica, Sulphur are important and required in larger quantities, also called **macro minerals**. Not to forget Sodium, an essential electrolyte maintaining the balance of water in and around cells, important for muscle and nerve function and maintaining a stable blood pressure.

Micro minerals or trace elements, for instance Copper, Manganese, Selenium, Iron, Iodine and many more have also specific biochemical functions in the body and should not be overlooked. They are required in much smaller doses, but they are just as important as macro minerals. Just like vitamins, minerals help the body grow, develop, and stay healthy. Our bodies use minerals to perform many functions from growing strong bones to transmitting nerve impulses and regulating the heartbeat. As an example, I remind readers of the importance of adequate amounts of iron needed in the body to ensure enough haemoglobin is available, a protein in red blood cells which carries the oxygen around the body.

The bioavailability of minerals is essential, here we remember the fact that plants have to digest those first to make them available to us as humans. Mineral deficiencies are very common in humans. It is said that up to 80% of people are mineral deficient. I am sure our pets would be in that category too when fed an artificial diet, not meat and bones. Dogs gain minerals from bones which is dissolved in their stomach. They have an extremely concentrated stomach acid, much more concentrated than ours. This serves two purposes: first this hydrochloric acid dissolves the bones of an animal and the minerals are set free to be taken up into the system. Secondly, the high concentration of the acid kills the many bacteria that the animal picks up with its prey. I bet there are many readers whose dogs burying their bones to eat them later with great relish.

I feel further explanation of certain essential minerals is in order. We all know the importance of **Calcium** in warm blooded animals, including humans of course. Calcium is the most abundant mineral in the body and the major component of bones and teeth, sustaining a healthy and strong skeleton. It is crucial to maintain an adequate level of calcium and its co-factors in the blood throughout life. Especially in childhood when bones are still growing. It is also important in old age, when bones can break down faster than they are able to be rebuild. Calcium is not just strengthening bones and teeth, it also helps to contract muscles, including the heart. It transmits nerve impulses, helps to activate blood clotting factors, moves blood through the veins and helps to stabilize and optimize proteins and enzymes in the body. In short calcium is vital for many functions in the body.

It is commonly thought that if we intake plenty of calcium, we will have strong bones. This is not necessarily so, not all of the calcium we consume will be absorbed. It depends on the source and the size of the molecule; it also has to be balanced with other minerals, trace elements and vitamins. Vitamin D and magnesium are calcium's friends as is potassium. They directly influence the absorption and metabolism of calcium within the body. So, it does not make much sense to take a calcium supplement alone because of advertising or someone told you to. All nutrients are reliant on each other to work in synergy, and all need to act together for a strong body.

Bone is an active tissue, despite its hard appearance. It consists of several different types of cells; among them, the *Osteoblasts* and *Osteoclasts* which are the most important ones. The *Osteoblasts* are responsible for the formation of bone, whereas the *Osteoclast* break down the bone. So, one can take lots of calcium supplement but still have bone diseases. Dairy offers a relatively low rate of absorption in contrast to leafy greens and fish bones like in anchovies or sardines. It is a misconception to believe that dairy makes strong bones. Looking at osteoporosis in Western Countries compared to Asian Countries. Asian people, at any age, suffer much less from osteoporosis than those of us in the West; despite drinking milk by the gallons for so called strong bones. When Asians migrate to Western countries, their lifestyle and choice of food changes and they often present with similar diseases as Europeans.

Magnesium should be mentioned in first place really. Magnesium deficiencies in people are so widespread and mostly overlooked. It definitely needs greater attention as another essential mineral for life. Magnesium is found in all cells of animals and humans and is necessary for many biochemical and enzymatic processes. Deficiency in Magnesium can be involved in all major health issues.

Magnesium and calcium are equally important for bone health.

About half of the amount of magnesium necessary is stored in the cells of organs and tissues. The rest is part of the Calcium/Phosphorus content of the bones; very little is dissolved in the blood. Magnesium is not easily stored in the body and needs to be ingested every day. It should be a supplement in every household, especially in a warm/hot climate, a must for people working outdoors and fitness fanatics. It is critical for heart health, muscle relaxation, and protein synthesis; it is anti-inflammatory and has many other functions. One of its largest roles is energy production within each cell. It certainly plays a critical role in brain function, and depression is often linked with deficiencies in magnesium. Even patients with diabetes benefit from supplementation. If you experience insomnia, magnesium is there to help. Taken in the evening it helps you sleep better by decreasing stress hormone levels and increasing the production of melatonin, the sleep hormone. One hears the complaint of restless legs quite often, especially when people get older - this is easily fixed with the right magnesium compound taken regularly.

Due to soil depletion, food processing and a diet mostly consisting of processed foods, deficiencies in magnesium are unfortunately common. Therefore, including more green, leafy plants in your daily foods will help. Magnesium is part of the chlorophyll molecule responsible for the green colour in plants. Apart from supplements, magnesium chloride can be applied to the skin as a transdermal application or adding Epsom Salts to your bath, both are easy and inexpensive ways to get a higher dosage into the body without having to deal with any laxative effects.

It truly is an amazing mineral and mood enhancer.

Potassium is the third most abundant mineral in the body and is just as essential as calcium and magnesium; the three actually work synergistically. It is required in high levels in the cells of humans and animals. It is important for heart health, and to balance fluid levels throughout the body. It is needed for good functioning of muscles and the nervous system; it is also required for enzymatic processes. Similar to magnesium it is found in green leafy plants.

The above three minerals, **Calcium, Magnesium** and **Potassium** belong to the **electrolytes**, (as well as **sodium** and **chloride**). In nutritional terms, this refers to essential minerals found in your blood, sweat and urine. Living and working in a hot climate or doing sport, electrolytes are necessary to keep the nervous system and muscles functioning. They also ensure the body's internal environment is optimal by keeping you hydrated and helping to regulate the internal pH. As important as it is for us humans to drink enough water when it is hot and/or when exercising, it concerns animals just the same. Dehydration and a loss of electrolytes can also happen to dogs when they lose more fluid than they are taking in. Water is absolutely critical to allow the cells to absorb nutrients, if left untreated, dehydration can cause serious organ damage and even death.

Dogs become lethargic, present with dry gums and a lack of skin elasticity if not drinking enough. They can be encouraged to take water by adding some juice from a sardine can or a little bone broth. If a pet is throwing up or has diarrhoea, it won't be resolved in one day. It is a good idea to be safe and call the vet. Especially for older pets or puppies or chronically ill animals it is crucial to ask for help when dehydration occurs. Please bear in mind, this is only a small representation of what is essential in an organism to stay healthy, there are many books and website available to learn more about what a human or animal body needs.

Now let's take a look at the dog food that is sold throughout the world.

Not that long ago, dogs were fed meat and bones or scraps from the kitchen. What happened? The last few hundred years with the advent of the industrial revolution, many people moved from country farms, small plots of land and villages into cities; this dramatically changed how we cooked and ate and where we got our foods from. It became easier to visit a shop to get our daily rations. This influenced the food industry to produce overly cooked, heavily processed and low-quality convenience foods, mostly laden with preservatives, chemicals, sugars etc. Unfortunately, the same foods have made their way into the food bowls of our pets. As a result, they are experiencing many similar health problems to humans. Buying tins and packets means one does not have to mess with fresh meat. It comes in neat packaging, and it lasts for a long time. I liken the pet food industry to the fast-food industry for humans. Both gained momentum in the last 50 years, unfortunately we now have the price to pay, more sick humans and pets than ever before.

McDonalds for humans and pets.

Vet practices are springing up everywhere to cater for all the sick pets. These animals are sometimes suffering from physical ailments like arthritis, diabetes, kidney failure, cancer, allergies and neurological disorders *before* they reach old age. There are also many who are experiencing anxiety, attention deficit disorder, ADD, and/or bad behaviour; the list gets longer each year. Does low quality or de-natured foods have anything to do with it? It certainly has. We know people on a fast-food diet present with similar symptoms, not to mention the weight problems in both people and pets. Toxins are also detected in pets' tissues, which is no surprise, they are exposed to the same environment as us. There are many studies looking at environmental toxins as well as household chemicals, and how they not only impact human health, but also that of cats and dogs. I will go into more about this in the next chapter.

As misguided as it seems to feed meat to a horse or a rabbit, it is equally misguided to assume that carnivores, like cats and dogs should be fed with grains, fruits, vegetables, and even dairy. Another fallacy is the idea that an all meat diet is lacking in vitamins and minerals. It is a fact; meat contains all the essential amino acids (building blocks of protein) and essential vitamins necessary for a carnivore. I have to admit, today's meat, unless it is organically grown, is full of antibiotics, herbicides and pesticides, and who knows what else, which also poses a problem - for everyone. Maybe it isn't so much that pet owners don't want to feed their pets properly. Many likely believe the advertising, by both manufacturers and vets that tell us, 'recommended premium food covers all of your dog needs'. So, it must be good for their pet, right? Vets, like human doctors, do not necessarily learn much about nutrition at university unless they have an interest in the subject. Unless they further educate themselves beyond their veterinary course, they probably don't have much idea about nutrients in foods. It is also a fact that pet food companies have a vested interest in the budding vets. They distribute information from their own research about the right nutrients for pets at universities; and of course, push it as a money-making product line for the student's future clinics.

I realize it might not be easy for some to accept that manufacturers and advertising can be shady and false. There are many books written, and internet sites created by concerned pet owners, pet magazines and some holistic vets, which verify what I am writing about. Obviously, living in a capitalistic age, money has to be made at all cost, and investors kept satisfied with returns. That doesn't guarantee the quality of a product. Many companies will use the cheapest, legally available ingredients, and governmental authorities often look the other way. Truthfully, the laws are lax and serve the industry to make a buck, regrettably, health or ethics don't often come into play. Despite claims of being balanced and nutritious they are anything but. Some ingredients are potentially harmful - sourced from slaughterhouses and rendering businesses. Even some of the so called premium or science foods aren't really much different, just more expensive. Reading the labels takes a few minutes.

Most of the large brands of pet foods comes from the US and some of their ingredients are imported from China. China has had a bad track record regarding foods, not only for pet food but also foods for human consumption. Profit is the bottom line. Even pet foods labelled made in Australia can have up to 50% foreign ingredients and still be labelled as 'made locally'. Even the website of the PFIAA, Pet Foods Industry Association Australia, does not state where the ingredients for pet foods come from. They declare on their website that dogs now need carbohydrates for energy; all of a sudden after thousands, more likely millions of years being meat eaters.

I am sure if pet owners knew what is in pet food, many wouldn't buy it. Most of us don't think of all the dogs, cats, horses and other animals that die every year, where do they go? Then there are the dead and diseased animals from zoos and farms which cannot be used for human consumption. Roadkill and slaughterhouse leftovers, dead chicken from farms and who knows what else. In my research, I also found articles revealing that the thousands of livestock who drowned in Hurricane Katrina in the US some years ago, went to rendering plants and eventually found their way into pet foods, unofficially. Rendering plants have been around for hundreds of years but we hardly see them or even hear of them. Everything mentioned above is rendered down in big boilers at over 100 degrees Celsius to kill pathogens. It is then spun in big centrifuges at high speeds so the tallow (fat) rises to the top and is removed. This tallow is later added to canned pet food. Opening a tin of standard pet food, one can often see the grease on top. The remaining mixture is dried and sold as meat meal to the pet food industry, specifically as a base to the dry food sold as kibble or pellets.

In many cases, animal fat includes meat sources from the 4-D class - defined as food animals that have been rejected for human consumption. This is because they were presented to the meat packing plant as Dead, Dying, Diseased or Disabled. High quality fats are expensive and not easily stored for any length of time. This makes them uneconomical to use in commercial foods/pet foods. Many of the animals used in the production are contaminated with pharmaceuticals, drugs, disinfection and cleaning agents which are used in slaughter houses, hooves, fur and feathers are also a part and one can't rule out chicken excrement mixed in with it.

Just in the last few years a drug called pentobarbital has been found in some brands of wet dog food in the USA, (not sure about Australia), which is used to euthanize cattle, horses, cats, dogs and other animals. Apparently, the FDA now acknowledges that the contamination of pet foods with this agent is widespread. Since the early 1990's this drug has been used by vets because it guarantees a quick death, with minimal discomfort to the animal. Unfortunately, the temperatures are not high enough in the rendering plants to destroy it. There are now lawsuits against some of the pet food manufacturers from pet owners who have lost their dog due to eating food contaminated with this drug. If this drug is found in pet foods, there is a chance many others are present too. It just isn't tested for anything else, so we do not know.

The pet food industry won't disclose their ingredients, for good reasons.

Thinking back to the Mad Cow Disease (BSE), which is a neurodegenerative disease and killed thousands of cattle, resulting from feeding them meat meal, (to a herbivore.) which was thought to have caused the contamination. It is a long story and can be researched, I just want to show what practices are applied all over the world. The industry has no scruples or ethics! It is so sad to see the big feedlots where thousands of cattle are crammed in a paddock and fed mostly manufactured food. I would like to point out the cruel ways of keeping those animals stresses them; not only physically but also emotionally, releasing hormones like adrenaline, cortisol and other steroids. We certainly ingest these when eating meat products and it is now thought those fear induced hormones may cause similar problems in humans.

A similar trick is used with fish. The residue of fish which is not used for other purposes consisting of heads, tails, fins, and innards are rendered and made into fish meal. Today, most fish are contaminated with mercury and the farmed fish are full of antibiotics and other drugs. They usually swim in their own excrement. In my opinion no one should eat farmed fish, not only because of the contamination, but also because of the cruelty to the creatures. The list goes on with cruelty to farm animals, pigs living for years in a small pen on metal grating, never see the daylight. Cattle in huge yards, standing in their own excrement, and so much more going on – just so we can eat cheap meat! Similarly, the hens existing in a tiny space on egg producing farms. After a few short years, exhausted from egg laying, they are made into meat meal.

When stated on top of the list on the packaging 'poultry or poultry by products' or 'meat' as pet food ingredient, one would assume that this is the main ingredient, unfortunately this is wrong. Just because it is on the top of the list does not mean it is the main ingredient. Advertising is allowed to split hairs when selling a product. Commercial dog foods mostly contain carbohydrates as fillers, they are cheap and easy to source. This can be corn, wheat, rice or any other grain, usually what did not pass inspection for human consumption. The contamination of grains with mycotoxins can have an adverse effect on humans and animals. Mycotoxins are substances produced by mould; aflatoxin as an example, is a well-known one growing on peanuts (which by the way, is a legume not a nut), but there are many other moulds possibly affecting any grain or vegetables when stored in warm and humid places.

Grains are the main part of nearly all dry foods and many canned foods as well. They are cheap and provide the bulk to make up the volume, but dogs can tolerate only a small amount, cats require a good source of meat, no carbohydrates at all. Does a carnivore eat grains in nature? No, occasionally they might pick up some seeds while eating grass but that would be minimal and not worth mentioning. The grains in herbivores stomachs are partly, or totally digested and so available to the carnivore as a digestive aid in form of good bacteria. All grains, unless from organic origins, are contaminated with herbicides, pesticides, and fungicides. Little if any testing or research is undertaken to examine the levels we and our pets ingest. Rice is theoretically a grain, but in a soft-boiled consistency it can be digested to some degree by dogs only, not cats. Brown rice would be the one to recommend, it contains some crude fibre and is energetically more balanced.

A note about refining grains, specifically wheat. Since the industrial revolution, wheat has been milled in high speed, stainless steel mills. They are fast and can produce so much more flour per day compared to stone milling. For hundreds of years, stone mills supplied people with whole grain, nutritious flour by milling the whole kernel and it was fresh as well. The modern process strips the goodness, the germ and the bran, from the kernel. All this leaves behind is empty carbohydrates, contributing to allergies and belly fat. What's more, the flour is stored for weeks or months at a time, carbohydrate devoid of nutrients, no good for anyone.

Wheat germ, the embryo of the kernel, rich in Vitamin E and the bran, valuable as fibre, are really an essential part of wheat and can be bought separately and added to foods.

Organic whole grain is always best.

Because of the issues with grain in pet foods, and pets getting allergies the same as humans, the industry has come up with another scam and advertises 'grain free' pet foods. People then assume the grain will be substituted with meat, but this not so. Other cheap fillers like beans, beet pulp (sugar), lentils, soybeans and other legumes and potatoes are used instead. Fava beans, also known as broad beans, have been in the news lately as a replacement of grains in pet foods. High in fibre, iron, complex carbohydrates and low in fat, they are considered nutritious for people, so why not use them in pet foods. The reason: because they are cheap. I suppose many people think what is healthy for us, and advertised as a biological agent replacing the grain, must be good for pets as well. Pet owners lack of knowledge is used by the industry to market inappropriate foods for cats and dogs.

Fava beans have been chosen over other legumes because they process well using a certain manufacturing process called extrusion. Most dry foods are made this way, using heat (up to 200 degrees C) and high pressure to force wet batches through a spiral shaped screw and at the end, the dried material is cut into required shapes. Heating up the ingredients to high temperatures further diminishes the nutritional value, a loss of more vitamins and minerals and protein denaturation, (destroying the molecular structure of proteins). Of course, it is an efficient method to ensure a long shelf life for the product. Apparently more important than the health of an animal! Human foods like snacks, cereals-based products, confectionary and hundreds more product lines are manufactured that way. Some compounds naturally occurring in legumes, are actually displacing the amino acids a carnivore's digestion is dependent on.

Research shows that the chemical reactions between the carbohydrates (sugar) and amino acids alters the micro biome, the essential bacteria needed to break down and absorb nutrients, causing the decline of taurine in the animal, dangerous especially for the health of cats. As I have mentioned a few times, cats need more protein in their diet than dogs and in comparison to puppies, kittens require 1.5 times more protein to grow up into healthy animals.

To me it is downright criminal that harmful chemical preservatives and other artificial additives are the norm in most pet foods. Colourings, sugar, salt, artificial flavourings, various types of additives and fillers in form of wheat, corn and soy flours are also added depending on the brand. Some are intentionally added by the manufacturer, while others, more toxic, stem from the herbicides, insecticides, and pesticides used by farmers to boost crop yields. Many pet foods advertised as 'preservative-free' do, in fact, contain preservatives. Cheap, artificially made vitamins are added which looks good on the ingredient list on the back of the packet. Even those are lost through the manufacturing process and so, are of little use to the animal. Within a short time, the organism is lacking vital components. The kind of minerals that are added to commercial dog foods are of inferior quality and their molecular size is too large to be of use to the cells. It should be supplied from natural sources.

The same scam used in human processed food to make it more palatable and entice the consumer to come back for more, has found its way into the manufacturing of pet food. Those additives are called *attractants* and are widely used in the industry. Foods made from highly processed ingredients and baked at high temperatures are tasteless, so smell/taste has to be artificially added to entice the animal to eat it. Looking at this scenario there is little doubt that deficiencies in daily feeds over time lead to symptoms and diseases.

A word about Dairy
Any kind of dairy foods are a definite ***no no*** for dogs and cats! I often hear "but cats have always drunk milk". This has been true at old style dairy farms or small farms milking their cows for private use. Farmers often provided a bit of fresh from the cow milk in the barn for the cats. Those cats weren't house pets like most cats of today. They lived around farms, catching mice and rats

and maybe other small animals. They lived mostly on fresh meat. The milk did not harm them for two reasons; the milk came straight from the cow containing the butterfat and, their natural diet of fresh meat kept them in good health. Unprocessed, real milk is still better than the stuff in bottles that has been adulterated by all kinds of processing and additives. It has even made into a long-lasting liquid - which I would not count as a food anyway.

Even for humans, I would not recommend cow's milk. The milk comes from lactating cows and contains growth hormones for the calf, which we certainly don't need. Bovine hormones are designed for calves to help them grow into adult cattle. It isn't only the hormones that are problem, lactose (milk sugar) in cow's milk causes many people stomach upsets because they lack an enzyme to digest it properly. Goat's milk is certainly better, the fat is more evenly distributed, so it is naturally homogenized. There is less lactose, more vitamins and minerals and the protein is more easily digested. New-born and young animals get everything they need from the mother's milk; and when weaned do not need any milk products.

Yoghurt is a bacterial fermentation of cows, goats or sheep milk and another product we should be carefully reading the label. Only yoghurts without any fruit or sugars are best, organic and made from a good strain of beneficial bacteria. These days there are coconut yoghurts in shops; they are just as good or even better, depending on taste, and great for anyone allergic to cow's milk. If the yoghurt is organic and natural, a smidgen might be beneficial to dogs in my opinion. If in doubt do not feed any.

We have now gone through all of the foods dogs and cats should not eat, so we progress to what is nourishing, healthy, and beneficial for them. At the same time, there is a chance to clean up human nutrition to improve our health. None of us are perfect, and always know what is right for the animal in our care, indeed for ourselves. There is always room to learn! We have so much information available today, not only about human health but also about animal health and wellbeing. More and more caring holistic vets around the world, are speaking out about the correct feeding and better physical care for pets. Many realize the damage done to pets by being fed a diet that lacks the appropriate nutrients. They have also come to understand that pets are being exposed to many toxins via skin applications, and also given internally. Not to mention the numerous vaccinations pet parents are talked into. It is time to counteract what the pet food industry churns out, promoting biologically inappropriate pet foods. Your dog or cat might survive ingesting these for some time, but they will not thrive. We have the power to turn this around and find better ways to nourish our pets.

> *The first choice we should make for our pet is not a rhinestone collar versus a plain one, but the proper food that keeps them healthy and well!*

There are many benefits of feeding a homemade diet to your pet, you are in control of ingredients and serve it with love and care. First, we have to clarify what we call fresh. Many packets and cans of both pet and human food items are labelled as containing fresh content. How can that be? Some ingredients might have been fresh before being processed, but once made into a product in a factory nothing is fresh anymore. The ingredients are exposed to high temperatures and various mechanical processes. Preservatives and other bits and pieces are then added to produce a saleable item with a long shelf life. Much money is spent on seductive advertising, so the consumer is totally overwhelmed and dazzled by fancy words.

There are certainly vitamins and minerals present in the original substance, and we can read the list on the packaging. What is left after processing and storing? To put it mildly, labelling foodstuff leaves a lot to be desired. In my view, there are downright lies in advertising, and this proves once again that profit comes before health. To be fair, and I am happy to say, there are some, (mostly smaller companies) that take care with processing their dog products; selling fresh meat, either frozen, in tins or dehydrated. Kibble dried at lower temperature is a less than good solution. I have tried to learn what temperature they are dried at from some companies that advertise better quality pellets. Unfortunately, all of them wanted to keep it a secret, for what reason I cannot guess. Nevertheless, their products are still better than a totally altered foodstuff from the large, mostly US based companies.
To retain the goodness of ingredients in dog pellets, provided they are mostly

meat, it is crucial that a drying temperature below 40 degrees Celsius, no higher is used, otherwise enzymes and water-soluble vitamins are destroyed.

Nearly 20 years ago I started a small business, making dog treats by drying meat, mostly liver (organic) mixed with a small amount of organic oats, minerals and herbs. This mixture was dried in a dehydrator at about 30° C, usually used to dry fruit at home. This treat was healthy, and every dog, and even many cats liked it. Anyone can make their own treats and dry them in the oven at very low temperatures. It is not as good as a dehydrator, but it works. ***Do not bake!*** To ensure added nutrients for dogs, I recommend cutting all kinds of sprouts into their meal, also a little bit of cooked pumpkin peels and finely grated zucchini for fibre is fine. The intestinal bugs need to be looked after and fed the right nutrients to do their work. More on this in chapter 7.

I resent all the dog treats - mostly made out of flour and baked at high degrees. They are very often presented in fancy shapes like cupcakes to entice humans to buy them. You will often find them sold at market stalls, and sometimes in pet shops. Feeding a pet is as simple as going to your butcher, getting some pet mince, fresh cheaper cuts of meat and bones. Pet mince is not a bad option as the butcher minces all kind of parts of a carcass, internal organs, small bones or whatever is left once the human fancy cuts have been removed. In my opinion this is better than just minced muscle meat, providing a variety of compounds necessary for carnivores. I suggest finding a reliable butcher to buy in bulk, he will surely tell you what goes into the mince.

We have the power to change the market by making the informed choices when we go shopping, letting manufacturing companies know we want a decent, healthy and nourishing product.

My Godson, Goldie

Chapter Six

Common Sense

What you think - you become
The Buddha

This chapter is about one of my favourite topics, common sense. Dictionaries explain it this way: *Your common sense is your natural ability to make good judgments and to behave in a practical and sensible way.* To me this means to observe everything, check the facts to determine if things can work out. Otherwise, I find new ways to get the job done or resolve the problem. I believe for every problem there is a simple and workable solution, as long as the solution is beneficial to everyone and environmentally friendly. The outcome of a situation also depends on the outlook we have in life and how we perceive a situation. A person who is down to earth, more in tune with the natural world and is self-reliant, will have a different perception of a given situation to someone who grew up in an authoritative environment and spent their life dominated by laws and regulations.

These days, so it seems, we rely mostly on what somebody said, especially when they have some sort of a title or are a so called authority, as well as the TV news or any other media or even what the neighbour said. Relying on too much information from the outside, and we are bombarded with it every minute, can be bewildering to anybody and downright confusing and possibly lead us along the wrong path. Unfortunately, the most common human response to confusion is apathy. Often when we are feeling unsure, we simply do nothing. A discerning, really, a critical attitude is essential so as not to get confused and see facts. Learning to distinguish between what makes sense for a better life for ourselves and our animals and what is just a gimmick by a company who wants to get money out of us, is a necessary exercise.

Are you living life or are you being lived?

It is very sad that vets often rely on research data produced by the pet food companies themselves. They frequently omit critical data that would show a not so favourable outcome, or perhaps the statistics are tampered with. It is a fact that it easy to fudge any statistics, numbers are easily shuffled around to get the result one wants. I also strongly resent the research done on dogs, cats and other animals. They are helplessly exposed to the cruelty of so-called scientific research. This does not mean we should become obsessed and worried about what makes sense and what doesn't. A good way to find the best outcome, is to make choices that are based on independent research and facts, as well as trusting our intuition. It is essential to keep cool and calm, even if the problem seems serious or our head space is full of worries. I personally find that in most cases, taking time, and relaxing in body and mind can have a positive turn and problems often resolve themselves. A great help is training our intuition, as discussed earlier, which can give us solutions to problems, sometimes even during sleep, and certainly assists us to navigate through life

Our pets give us so much pleasure - not to mention a boost for our ego. They love us unconditionally and serve us - not expecting much in return. We, as carers and guardians, should feel honored and privileged that they trust us and provide for them as best as we can. I deliberately omit the word owner, as I believe we do not own anything, everything is only borrowed for the time we are here, and we certainly don't own a friend. More and more people are beginning to realize the bond they have with their pet, and the responsibility they have to live up to. It is becoming more widely accepted that animals (plants as well and I believe any matter on this planet really), have their own consciousness, understanding of the world and themselves. So, I feel it is a priority to do the best we can regarding their health and wellbeing, which really backfires in a positive way, keeping ourselves in good shape as well.

Much depends on the common sense in daily life.

Certainly, most people recognize how much of our environment is in dire straits and needs cleaning up. I am going to list some problem zones in our immediate surroundings, often encroaching our lives from the greater environment of Australia, other continents and even the planet as a whole. No continent is separate from any other, we are connected by the upper atmosphere, wind, sea currents, the sun - and these days by pollution as well!

I am sure everyone is familiar with **Gaia**, the name of our Earth, called by many native peoples, Mother Earth. In 1979, James Lovelock defined Gaia as: *"A complex entity involving the Earth's biosphere, atmosphere, oceans, and soil; the totality constituting a feedback or cybernetic system which seeks an optimal physical and chemical environment for life on this planet."* He named our home after Gaia, the primordial goddess who personified the earth in Greek Mythology. The Earth is a living, breathing, sentient organism. Holistically, Earth is a living entity of its own, maintaining conditions necessary for her own and of course her inhabitants' survival. No longer can we think of separate parts of the Earth, whatever happens on the planet like deforestation, increase of emissions, pollution of the land and the seas by plastics, monocultures of crops, we are all involved.

We depend on common sense of all the world's citizens.

Soil Health

Let's start with our own backyard first. Cities are worse than country areas in regard to air pollution. On the other hand, the majority of the farming community destroys the soil with herbicides, pesticides, artificial fertilizer and who knows what else. This certainly doesn't mean that suburban gardens are the healthiest places. I have been to many homes and haven't found one that doesn't have any of the above-mentioned sprays in the garden shed. Glyphosate seems to be everywhere, despite the common knowledge that it is a poison to all organisms.

It wasn't that long ago when it was normal to chip or pull some weeds, these days people think they have to be poisoned. Of course, this doesn't require much physical exertion and saves time. But then, because of the lack of exercise, we take the time to go to the gym to keep the muscles in some sort of shape. In the meantime, the poison soaks into the earth, inhibiting the growth of the micro-organism, earthworms and everything else necessary for a healthy soil. If it rains it is carried through the drains into rivers and seas.

Soil health is our wealth!

Healthy, fertile soils contain an immense diversity of microorganisms, which directly contribute to the biological fertility of that soil. In addition to fertility, soil microorganisms also play essential roles in the nutrient cycles that are fundamentally important to life on the planet. These organisms are responsible for the plant's uptake of nutrients, which in turn provide not only humans but all other animals with the nutrients, the building blocks necessary for health. Soil fertility is dependent on three interacting and interdepending components, which are *physical, chemical* and *biological fertility*. The *physical* refers to the properties of the soil like its structure, texture, water absorption and holding capacity. *Chemical* fertility involves the nutrients in the soil like minerals, also the acidity or alkalinity and salinity which would be harmful to the plants. The *biological* fertility obviously refers to the organisms that live in the soil, interacting with each other and performing many vital processes. The richer the diversity of the biological organisms such as bacteria, viruses, fungi, and algae that form the interactive communities, the better the soils. We certainly are familiar with earthworms, a good indication of a vital soil. Many more important components are in a healthy soil not mentioned here, but available to be studied in books and articles.

The topsoil is where all plants first germinate. Their roots then penetrate further into the earth into deeper layers, harvesting the minerals and trace minerals made available by microbes. These are most important for growing our food. Soil microbes are responsible for breaking down plants, decomposing any organic matter and re-cycling nutrients. Without those microbes we would not have any soil at all. Life as we know it would not be possible. To generate a few centimetres of topsoil can take up to 1000 years, so it is sad to realize the losses of useable, fertile soil through bad agricultural practices, overloading with chemicals foreign to the earth and overstocking with animals.

We cannot put enough emphasis on a healthy, vital soil teeming with life.

There are certain factors that have played a key role in declining nutrient values in foods since about a hundred years ago. The start of mechanized farming has much to answer for, using heavy machinery to compact soils, disturbing the upper layer of land by ploughing too often where most of the microorganisms live, application of artificial fertilizers, then the use of pesticides, and some years ago the introduction of engineered plants and glyphosate. A residue of the sprays is mostly found on the lawns, foot paths around the home and in the streets, a danger especially to children who play there, as well as to pets walking there and later licking their paws or eating grass and ingesting it that way.

Everybody has heard about the controversy of the weedkiller, Round Up, a non-selective herbicide and its implication of high toxicity for all life. There has been a dramatic increase in its use in recent years. This has resulted in a rise in cancers, and many other diseases in humans and pets. In the last few years, it has been found everywhere on the planet, specifically its main compound, glyphosate.

Round Up was registered in the US in 1974 by Monsanto. Its active ingredient is an organo-phosphorus compound, glyphosate, which acts by inhibiting certain enzymes in plants and so kills them. Round Up is really a toxic cocktail, made up of several substances. I explain this in length because it is found all over the planet in most foods, for humans and animals alike. American studies some years ago show it is now found in mothers' milk, what's more their levels are ten times higher than that of European women. Europe has stricter laws, also regarding fluoride as a poison, and some countries are now looking into prohibiting Round Up. In recent years more people claiming their cancers are caused by Round up and court cases against the big companies are on the rise.

Grains like sorghum, corn, wheat, oats, barley, rice and many other staple foods are contaminated. Much of it is fed to cattle and other farm animals, eventually ending up on our table. Not only are the crops sprayed when growing, they are also dowsed with glyphosate just before harvest, so they die and dry before harvesting. This is called desiccating and it is practiced in many countries, especially when there has been a wet year, and harvesting the crops in wet weather would be a problem. This desiccation practice is also allowed for lentils, peas, rye, buckwheat, millet, sugar beets, potatoes and sunflowers. It increases the profitability for the farmer, and we eat foods laden with toxins.

I just want to talk about fava beans again, I mentioned in Chapter 5, they are currently the fillers for dry pet kibble, substituting for wheat in so called wheat free kibble. A filler is a cheap substance to make up the bulk of food items. Fava beans are exposed to this desiccation process with glyphosate as well as being sprayed with herbicides while growing. Pets certainly get their dose of poison from this as well. There is another important fact I think everyone should know about. I mentioned earlier glyphosate inhibits certain enzymes in plants, it also disrupts gut bacteria in mammals, killing the beneficial forms, causing an overgrowth of pathogens - the bad ones, hence affecting the immune system. One doesn't have to study rocket science to see the connection between the increase in digestive complaints and poisoned basic foods. So why do we still have farming practices that supply us with toxin laden food? It doesn't take much explaining - because of profits!

We are bewitched by materialism.

Those huge companies make millions, eventually leaving behind soils devoid of life with their practices. Killing the microscopic bacteria our food plants needed to transform minerals into acceptable compounds for digestion, and then having to use artificial fertilizers on those leached out soils. Of course, they sell the fertilizer as well. To be able to spray crops with this herbicide, some of our most widely grown grains had to become resistant. Monsanto patented the seeds of the most common grains and vegetables which had to be genetically modified to survive the toxic spray. Slogans like 'GMO's are saving the world from hunger' turned out to be false, of course. Many farmers, especially in poorer countries, have lost income after using poisons for some years, resulting in dwindling harvests common in countries like India. Those big companies think they can trick nature by genetically changing what has for hundreds of thousands of years been manufactured by nature.

It is stupidity to poison the soil, and in turn ourselves and animals.

Soil health leads to Nutritious Foods
Due to soil depletion, crops grown decades ago were much richer in vitamins and minerals than what we get today. It is a fact that even organically grown vegetables and fruit have less nutrients than say 50 years ago. Modern intensive farming methods have stripped increasing amounts of nutrients from the soil in which our food is grown. It is sad to say that each successive generation of vegetable is less nutritious than the harvest before. I found a study by the US Department of Agriculture comparing the nutritional value in vegetables and fruit from 1950 and 1999. It shows a decline in proteins, calcium, phosphorus, iron, B and C and E vitamins, and most likely a decline in magnesium and zinc as well. The decline in nutrients is blamed on agricultural practices designed to improve size, growth rate and pest resistance of crops - not the nutritional value. There is more effort put into breeding new varieties of crops to provide greater yield and a better climate adaptability than taking care of the nutritional content of crops.

Let us not forget that food isn't just the sum of its nutrients; it is a complex package of life-giving compounds. It profoundly influences our physical, metabolic, emotional and behavioural part of our make-up. Fruits, vegetables, herbs and spices contain a complex mixture of many different parts; amongst them, phytonutrients, benefitting health and wellbeing. Harvesting and eating fresh within a short time, supplies us with a fantastic nutritional value. Not so long ago, our ancestors ate what they picked from the garden on the same day; not what was in the fridge for a week.

Phytonutrients are said to be a part of the plants immune system, offering protection against bacteria, fungus, and other parasites. So far, only a few of the thousands of phytonutrients have been isolated and tested. They range from being antioxidants, anti-inflammatory agents and are immune supportive, regulate hormones and so much more. Phytonutrients are different from vitamins, minerals or macro nutrients and found in vegetables, fruits, any herbs and even spices. They even appear in edible flowers and give colour to many fruits and vegetables. A good example are the blueberries highly regarded for their phytonutrient content, supporting eye health amongst other things, a fantastic antioxidant. Carrots contain the well-known carotenoid, the yellow colour. Even olive oil and foods like garlic and onions are high in those nutrients.

As humans we are all somewhat different in our physical make up. Not only the continent and race we are born into matters, but also the diets our forebears ate, all affected our DNA. Looking into Ayurvedic Medicine, which has been practised for thousands of years in India, and like Chinese Medicine has influenced Holistic Health in the West, they focus on balancing the energies using diet and herbs, as well as the right life style and right thinking. When there is minimal stress, the body's natural defence systems will be strong and can more easily defend against diseases. An Ayurvedic diet is prescribed accordingly to our unique constitution, called the Doshas, to adjust our inner balance, lead to wellbeing and to reduce stress. Great emphasis is put on clean, fresh, and unadulterated foods, herbs and spices suited to each person's constitution and health level. Occasionally we see the catch phrase 'eat a rainbow diet', a great idea supplying us with a variety of vegetable and fruit, full of phytonutrients, not only energizing the body, but also having a positive effect on our mood and levelling out emotions. I bet it enhances the spirit as well.

There are many studies of junk food addicts and their change in behaviour, their decline in not only physical, but also mental health. In my opinion it is plain to see that those de-natured foods, often with artificial ingredients, and high in salt and sugar, contribute to obesity, heart disease, diabetes, fatty liver, probably influence certain cancers and generally let people age earlier. As the physical health and level of energy drops, depression and mood swings are on the rise. Junk food isn't only made for people, commercial pet foods are in the same category.

Not all is lost.

There are many groups, not only in the country areas but also in the cities, growing vegetables on nature strips, vacant lands and even on roof tops. A few years ago, I heard of multi-story buildings in New York, Sweden and other countries, specifically built for plants, may they be vegetables or other green plants to improve the air in cities. Vertical gardens are on the rise as well; the advantage is they can be added on to existing buildings, commercial or private. Any bare wall can be beautified by a vertical garden, and fresh food can be gained as well. I have seen vertical gardens, even small ones, in cafes and spas, enhancing the premises, and to top it off, they can harvest a few fresh herbs or flowers. It is even a water saving exercise as the water is recycled and used again. Picking vegetable and fruit from one's own garden and serving it that day is such a satisfying feeling. Even pots on a balcony are great to grow herbs, a few lettuces or snow peas, and not to forget to plant some flowers as well - especially the edible ones. I have always grown my own sprouts, easily done in the kitchen near a window. There are a variety of seeds available, Alfalfa being the most common ones, however many others are great too. Broccoli, radish, red clover, lentils, sunflower just to name a few, are easy to sprout and delicious to eat.

There is also the issue about waste, especially bio waste from the kitchen. Not everyone has a garden or room for a proper compost bin, but there are ways around it. Small composters are available from garden supplies, the size of large buckets, great for any space. Better still is a worm farm but that needs a small outdoor space in the shade. Just recently I came across a pet poo waste system which is fantastic for small backyards, especially if there are several pets, may they be dogs, cats, rabbits or birds. All these small composting systems work with enzymes which must be added to eat the scraps, miraculously turning them into fertile soil. Even coffee grounds and tea leaves are perfect for pots and the garden, as well as eggshells either mixed into a compost heap or dissolved in a little vinegar.

We know from *Masaru Emoto's* research and books about the *Messages of Water* that our thoughts, caring attitude and attention certainly has an influence on the formation of water crystals. So why wouldn't this happen with food? Ever thought why homemade food tastes better than restaurant food? Apart from fresher ingredients, it is the caring and loving preparation of meals we taste when eating, and our positive attitude improves digestion. People used to pray before meals and give thanks. To me this has nothing to do with religion. Whenever we approach with caring thoughts and feelings, it is felt by everything, may that be plants, animals, humans, food or even my laptop. Put love and good intentions into everything you consume or use, as this will have a direct effect on your physical body.

> *Place a piece of paper with a loving message written or a heart drawn on it under your pet's dishes. It will certainly enhance their food and water and improve digestion.*

With the busy and money-driven lifestyle we have today, we forget what kind of effect our thoughts can have on our health and everything around us. So be mindful before you eat or drink water, feed your pet or do anything else for that matter. It is vital to appreciate the plants that grow for us and nourish us.

Control the market, choose wisely

We are the 99%; the public controls what is being made and sold by our choices. If we, as consumers don't buy any inferior, contaminated or worthless products, they will stop being made. It is up to us to check out each item and make wise, informed choices about what is good and beneficial for us and our pets. Basic foods do not cost much, therefore they are not very interesting for the large companies. There is not much profit to be made there. We have to differentiate between **minimally** and **maximally** processed products. The minimally processed foods are items like bagged lettuces, vegetables already cut for convenience or roasted nuts which would still be good items to eat.

Maximally processed foods include cooked, canned, frozen, other foods that gone through a process to preserve or fortify them in any way. I am sure anyone would agree, anything that has gone through any process is less valuable for us to eat. This is not such a drama when used sparingly and the majority of one's food is fresh but poses a risk when used daily. Even when eaten occasionally, I am sure a less robust person is likely to have nutrient deficiencies. It has been suspected for a long time and has been substantiated by research in the last few decades with convenience foods on the rise, that processed foods make us fat, and eventually sick. The high content of carbohydrates, salt and sugar, bad fats, lack of fiber and many other additives foreign to a human body, definitely contribute to the rise in obesity, heart problems, diabetes and so on. Unfortunately, not only the physical body is affected but also the emotional part of us.

The added worry is the packaging. Plastics and tins lined with plastics leach chemical compounds into the foods, and we do not know whether any foreign chemicals happen to contaminate the products while going through the processing line. Human beings have a body designed to eat a variety of fresh foods every day. Our physical bodies have not mutated over thousands of years, nor have they changed in any way to become healthy by consuming altered and foreign products.

As humans, we do need a species correct diet as well.

Talking about canned foods, I would like to mention canned sardines which are a good source of protein and providing bio available calcium from the bones of the fish, soft enough to be digested. One has to be vigilant and read labels as to ascertain that they are sustainably fished, the same goes for tuna. They are good to eat but these days many fish around from every ocean are polluted with mercury and micro plastics. I also avoid fish grown in fish farms as I mentioned in an earlier chapter, they are contaminated with antibiotics and possibly other chemicals. It is important to realize that wild fish obtain their omega 3 from aquatic plants or other fish. In aquaculture, they are fed with soy, corn and other stuff foreign to a fish species. Although some breeds can survive on those grains, others cannot. Tuna and salmon need some fish protein to stay alive, so smaller fish like sardines, are caught to extinction to feed the aquacultures around the world. Larger fish, for instance some whale species and sharks are dependent on those sardines. Due to the artificial feed, the flesh of the salmon is more of a grey colour instead of pink, which is not appealing to customers. To counteract this, the salmon is fed colour, so they look like the real ones caught in the ocean. In nature, salmon feed off shrimp and krill which contain carotenoids giving them their particular colour.

,

Apart from the contamination which also poses a problem for our health, the fish are highly stressed, like all animals and humans confined to small spaces. This stress situation predisposes the animals to a lowered immune system which leaves them wide open to parasite infections, like sea lice, possibly spreading to and infecting other wild fish. To combat the infestations, operators dump high amounts of antibiotics into the sea, damaging other sea life. A similar problem posed by the amount of excrement from millions of fish contained in a small space. I suggest checking with the fish monger or inquire at the supermarket about the origin of the fish. Don't be fooled if you read 'Atlantic Salmon' on the label, you may think it comes from the Atlantic Ocean, but nearly all salmon are farm raised.

Frozen foods are next in line, which keeps food safe over long period of time by delaying spoilage and preventing the growth of micro-organism and enzymes, especially when kept under -18 degrees. Fortunately, most micro-organisms survive being frozen, but care has to be taken when defrosting. It is advisable to use foods immediately when thawed out. We have to distinguish between freezing foods at home or commercially in factories. In itself, frozen foods are not such a bad idea, surplus fruits and vegetables if snap frozen when ripe are fantastic and can be enjoyed in times when they are not available. This is great for home gardeners or even small farms and is usually done as contact freezing. Luckily, freezing has very little effect on nutrients, especially when frozen at peak condition, not long after harvest, compared to fresh vegetables and fruit when transported and stored for a length of time.

Commercially, some vegetables may be blanched; as a result, they lose some of the water-soluble vitamins. There are a few different methods used in commercial freezing, depending on the product. I am talking only of fresh frozen vegetables, not prepared meals. Not much is known about the preparation in the factory for those. There is hardly any vitamin loss from freezing meat. However, during defrosting there is a loss of vitamins contained within the liquid, unless that is used as well. Defrosting pet meat is easy, either take a packet out of the freezer the day before and thaw in fridge or when in a hurry place it in warm water.

The choices we make today, will be our future tomorrow.

Avoid plastics

I touched on the problem of plastics earlier; it has been such big problem for so many years. In my lifetime, we have inundated the planet with many different plastics. From tiny items to bottles and bags, foam and many other kinds of articles are polluting our home and environment. A good example are the shopping bags, after years of pollution, shops and customers are finally being discouraged to use them. Unfortunately, they have not totally taken them off the market - as should have happened. These days, the media are sharing more about the damaging effects of any kind of plastics. Hopefully, more people are taking notice. There have been many studies, but most of it isn't the eight o'clock news. The name plastic is a broad term and really started to emerge around the second world war. The majority of it is synthesized from oil, coal, gas and other chemicals. It causes pollution when being manufactured, as well as producing harmful gases when burned or poisoning the ground when dumped in landfills. Some of it takes hundreds of years to decompose. Plastics really are a curse of our time!

We hear about recycling plastics which has been an effort by some industries to reduce our waste. Since all plastic items are distinct in their combination, they have to be separated and different methods applied to recycle. It is not a long-term solution. Tinned food came on the market in the early nineteenth century, after experimenting with different techniques and metals. Today, the cans are made of steel, and are coated inside with a polymer. The canning process has several stages. Cleaning the vegetable in tanks of water or under high pressure, then they are peeled and cut before blanching them in hot water. This not only softens the fiber but also de-activates the enzymes, an important and life-giving part of plants. As mentioned before, tinned food is okay as an emergency standby, but not something that should be consumed every day.

The packaging industry tells us that the lining of the tins has been changed in recent years because the problem chemical, *Bisphenol A*. It has been found in most food stuffs, leaching out from the lining inside the tins. Then BPA free became trendy. The substitutes weren't any better because the basic structure stayed the same. Obviously, some sort of lining is necessary otherwise the metal of the tins would corrode. I checked the website of the Can Manufacturer Institute, and they state that the lining of cans is made from acrylic and polyester these days. Apparently, this has been extensively tested. I personally do not believe *any* chemical is good for us. The good news is, there are more items made from natural fibers. One only needs to ask or look for them in supermarkets. It is worth it!

While it isn't possible to avoid plastics altogether,
we can look for alternatives!

Chapter Seven

Help for Self-Help

All that is gold does not glitter, and not all that wander are lost.
J.R.R. Tolkien, the Fellowship of the Ring

Our lives are mostly conditioned by someone else's ideas, laws, and regulations. We are constantly bombarded with warnings 'unless we behave this way or think that' something unpleasant or even dangerous might happen. This leaves us little time to go inward and gain clarity about our existence. We are told unless we follow such and such orders or apply particular ideas, we won't be happy and well. Ultimately, everyone wants a calm and uncomplicated life to express his or her dreams and purpose. This can only happen when we de-program ourselves from dogma, start believing in ourselves, and follow our hearts intelligence.

This does not mean we should have a 'never mind' attitude if we experience opposition or problems. As I see it, and have certainly experienced myself, we attract certain issues in life so we can learn from them and eventually solve them. Sometimes we have to repeat the scenario before we recognize the issue. Unless we recognize that there is a problem, a solution is hard to come by. Problems in life can make us a better person, they can help us get to know ourselves - who we are, what makes us tick, and how we react to life's surprises. Usually called problems, I see them as challenges, even as opportunities to grow; they are definitely a part of our life. Most people tend to be afraid or uncomfortable and wish the problem would go away. They feel they have to come up with a solution immediately, look for someone to fix it or blame the circumstances, or sometimes, other people.

Firstly, the problem needs to be recognized with a clear mind and analysed, its symptoms looked at and accepted. Unless we accept that there is a challenge, we cannot find a good solution. It is also good advice to calm down, relax and take time to think. Most of us act according to our comfort zone, we actually become addicted to that state. This addiction is based on the chemicals released from our brain by having the same thoughts or doing the same thing as we have done many times before. This means repeating the past unconsciously, we discussed this in an earlier chapter. Unfortunately, we will come across unpleasant behaviours by others at times. Accusations, something that affects us in a negative way or makes us angry and provokes a reaction. Quite often, we lash back and try to get even or stew in it.

In colloquial terms it is called 'pushing ones' buttons.

The answer is just to keep cool and realize we are all each other's teachers. In my clinical hypnotherapy sessions with clients who sought relief from an addiction or habit, I ask them to remove all (the imaginary) buttons so no could press them and cause the usual reaction. For many it worked well but requires a conscious attitude and patience. Very often these reactions are based on families, tribal and cultural values, a subconscious fear of not being accepted or being afraid of severing ties with close people. Shame and trauma can also come into play. Thinking about the actions we take every minute is paramount. We should not just repeat patterns in life taken on from our peers; nor should we cling to ideas someone told us to follow. It is not easy to break these cycles which often have been established for many generations. They are stored not only in our bodies cell library, but also in human morphic fields without us even thinking or knowing about.

Looking at the world today, I believe now is the time for everyone to become conscious of every thought, decision and action in every minute of our existence. In short, we all need to be responsible. Big changes are happening, very big changes; not only around us, but in our own lives also. Resilience is necessary to bounce back and embrace new ideas to carry on in a caring and responsible way, looking after ourselves and our furry family members. I have written the above to make it easier for the reader to recognize the rut we are all in and how our daily lives have become a product of an artificial environment created by politics and the industry far removed from our needs, companies with often false advertising and of course the media which in most cases does not tell facts, only pushing someone's agenda. It is high time to change our ways, ease the burden on the planet, honour nature.

Self-help number 1: Be mindful at all times

It is often thought mindfulness is like a meditation. These terms have become more known in the Western World in the last 80 years. There are many similarities between the two and they can overlap but are not exactly the same. There are many types during meditation: Mantra based meditation, when a mantra or wise words are repeated, visualisation meditation, guided meditation, calming one's mind meditation, sound meditation and others. It is an intentional practice, focusing inwardly, usually starting with deep breathing and bringing the awareness to the breath. Then guiding the mind to a certain focus and tuning inward. The time spent in meditation could be 10 minutes or several hours. The best time is early in the morning or in the evening when winding down from a day's work. Getting 'lost' in the garden, as some gardeners would know, swimming in the sea, even being absorbed in a certain kind of work you enjoy, is similar to a meditation.

Mindfulness is all about being aware, noticing and paying attention to thoughts, emotions and actions during waking time and the effect we have on our surroundings. It really is the simple act of paying attention, involving all senses and being aware of thoughts. It can certainly be difficult for us humans to stay in the present moment. Studies found that we spend most of our waking hours thinking about something other than what we are engaged with. I am sure we all know this about ourselves. We often spend our thoughts on regrets (focused on the past) and worrying about the future - which hasn't even happened. Mindfulness means being present in *all* situations. Our animals are always present in the now. This is what our pets do best, being here and now, not getting lost in worries and thought. This is something we can certainly learn from our four-legged friends!
Being mindful in daily life helps us to see clearer. It helps us to gain more clarity about who we are, and the role we play in the here and now. We also realize the responsibility we have to ourselves and everything else when we are present in the here and now. It is certainly a step towards a greater

appreciation of the planet we live on. In the last 200 years, we have done more damage than the thousands of years before. It is time to stop the abuse of the earth and its non-human inhabitants. This change can only start when each person is being conscious and mindful about their life, and their role in it.

Don't set limits!

There have been wise teachers on this earth who left much wisdom behind. We are fortunate today to have many books and talks readily available, not only by ancient teachers but also by our contemporary wise humans. Looking back in history it wasn't the norm for 'common people' to be taught to read. We should be glad that the opportunity to learn is provided to us. I firmly believe we are here to learn, to gain momentum, to be the best we can be, to understand nature, the cosmos and, of course, to understand our pets. In my opinion, we have been given the internet to learn from each other, to share knowledge and connect. There are many websites by responsible people sharing their research, experience and wisdom, I find it uplifting to listen to wise words on a daily basis. I certainly would advise being discerning and careful about who you trust, make sure you do your research.

We have the capacity to look at our current daily life. We can decide if what we do is helpful and engaging or destructive to others and/or the environment. Once we realize what a miracle we are, physically and spiritually, we learn to respect and take care of ourselves and our actions first, then of others and the environment we live in. Quantum Physics and Energy Medicine have opened new fields and provided explanations of the amazing capabilities of the New Human that has emerged. Sometimes, we just don't realize that fact within ourselves. Recognizing this strength in us proves to be a basis for a growing confidence in our decisions. It can open up the path to intuiting the world around us, eliminating the need to rely on orders or haphazard ideas from others. It follows that the environment and the pets in our home benefit from our mindfulness, self-confidence, and wise choices to provide the best care for the animal in our lives.

Ideas to put into practice:

- After waking up, start deep breathing consciously relaxing, and just let thoughts pass by. 10 minutes of meditation, (longer if you can), focusing on gratitude for everything in our lives is great.
- Be mindful after getting out of bed. Feel the water in the shower, notice how you are brushing your teeth, be present in whatever routine you follow in the morning.
- Practicing with everyday activities, mindfulness soon becomes a habit, noticing even the small things. In time, we will become calmer, more focused and have a more relaxed attitude towards daily matters.
- Greet your pet and observe how happy he or she is to see you. No matter how you look or how you are dressed, appreciate their presence in that moment with you. They will feel your gratitude, and in return boost your mood to start the day in a positive way.

Can we expect the world to change if we don't change ourselves?

Self-help number 2: Health starts in the head

In my clinical situation, it dawned on me a long time ago to look at the thought processes of people regarding health and wellbeing. When asked the question: "Do you take care of yourself?", most will answer "Yes, of course I do!". But when followed with "In what way?" the tricky part begins. We have not been taught how to care about ourselves properly. We often feel if we eat fairly well and take a walk occasionally, or even go to the gym once a week, all seems to be well. Self-care is an activity done deliberately to take charge of our physical, mental, and spiritual needs; as well as balancing our emotions, having an uplifting outlook on life, and keeping anxiety and worry at bay. It really is a simple concept, but a conscious one which is often overlooked. It is the key to a good relationship with oneself and others, and certainly a recipe for a well lived and healthy life. It is a concept we have to find for ourselves, with the help of a health professional if needed. One should make a commitment to do the best for oneself.

So, we need to look more closely at health, and what we can do about it in a toxic and unsafe environment. I invite you to pay special attention to *survive* versus *thrive*. There is a huge difference between the two states of health. I am sure everyone would like to be healthy, but many of us just survive. I hear people often say, "I haven't got much time to think about and do all of these things".

Health is not just the absence of disease.

As mentioned in earlier chapters, all our experiences and thoughts have an effect on our physical lives. They are actually in charge of our body, unless conscious and authentic thinking is practiced. I would like to point out that only authentic thoughts bring about change. It was fashionable through the 'new age' movement to have notes pasted everywhere with our affirmations. It rarely worked because we wrote down what we wanted, but weren't aware that they were only wishes, more like superficial thoughts. Only authentic thoughts, coming from deep within, from the heart, from our soul or our spirit can bring about positive changes.

This is how animals live, authentically and honestly in the present.

Structures have built up from habits and patterns as we go through the day. We mostly move through life on autopilot because it easier to do the same thing today that we did yesterday. Thoughts and emotion are less beneficial; worries, fear and grief influence our metabolism in a detrimental way, leaving us wide open to physical changes in the body. As happens to a chain when strong force is applied, the weakest link breaks first; very similar to what happens with an organism. As a result of those negative thoughts and emotions, our metabolism changes to predispose our particular bodily makeup to certain symptoms and eventually diseases. We manufacture stress hormones as a result of the discrepancy between what we want to experience, and what actually happens.

The stress output is not likely to be great when we expect sunshine next weekend on our visit to the beach and it rains. This dramatically changes when situations exist like grief of losing a partner or other loved ones, being physically or psychologically attacked, a life-threatening scenario, a diagnosis of severe illness and even perceived threats. All of these situations, and many others, have an output of stress hormones. I would even count the negative news in the media as a stressor. By listening and watching them daily, we become desensitized and are often in a constant, even if minor, stress situation without noticing it happening. Gory movies showing cruelty to humans and animals, affect all of us, especially children.

It is easy to forget that our pets pick up on our emotional state. They are exposed to the vibrational situation dominant in our homes. This can be a happy and relaxed situation but also can be anxious and worrisome. Especially when we are constantly bombarded with bad news or incessantly urged to buy this or that article. Healing physical ailments is a natural and normal functioning of the body, stress hormones hinder the body from healing itself. Animals do this naturally, unless we put them in certain situations where they can't help themselves, which diminishes their inherent capabilities. As a part of the natural world, as our pets are, we can watch them and learn to relax and de-stress like they do. Cats are the best example, they have the knack to instantaneously relax, switch off and sleep. This does not mean we need to sleep as many hours as a cat, but it is a fact that sleep plays a vital role in good health and wellbeing throughout life. Getting enough quality sleep at the appropriate time is an important biological function, essential for life and certainly for a good mood.

While we sleep, many significant functions take place. These help the body in physical recovery and repair, supporting brain development, cardiac function and metabolism. It also supports the learning process and helps to improve memory. Naturally, babies and children need much more sleep than adults. In older age it can vary, but generally a good and refreshing sleep contributes to a vital and enjoyable day. Needless to say, the same applies to very young and older animals as well. I believe we humans have just as much potential to fulfill our role as any other species. We strive for the same health and wellbeing as anyone else on the planet.

Self-help number 3: Choice is a power tool

We need to choose products carefully. Not only food and how we prepare it, but also everything we use in our homes, cosmetics, cleaning products, clothing, plastics of any kind, garden sprays and fertilizer. Unless biodegradable and free of toxins, most are detrimental to our wellbeing and also poison the soil, groundwater and waterways. Many of the common products we use, accumulate in our organs and tissues unless moved out of the body. This may lead to cellular damage, inflammation, chronic diseases, and premature aging. It is important to be aware of the cumulative effect of all those substances.

Let's start with foods, and how we can take charge of them. They are one of the main ingredients in life. We need to put a plan into place to stay healthy and energetic in our contaminated world. Everything doesn't have to be changed at once. Perhaps start by buying some 'clean' foods from the organic shelf at the supermarket, a health food shop or a fresh local market. There are many weekend markets where farmers or local people sell their surplus vegetable and fruit. Seasonal produce grown locally is always best; not only because of the freshness and supporting local people, but the foods grown where you live have a similar energetic signature. It also good to eat according to the seasons as nature intended. Seasonal nutrients help us to grow and stay healthy.

It is the freshness in produce that benefits us. A short transportation ensures that fruits and vegetables can be picked when ripe. This is far better than produce shipped from other countries - which must usually be harvested while still firm and green. These products are usually refrigerated, frozen or irradiated to survive the travel time, especially across international borders. Buying local guarantees ripeness, a higher vitamin content, less pollution, and less packaging. The added bonus is you can check if it is sprayed or really organic with a local grower. You can also establish a connection with the farmer to make your voice heard and hold him more accountable. Customers can have a direct impact on the local supply chain, this is generally difficult or not possible with the large supermarkets. Putting a face to the seller of the product might encourage consumers to change their buying habits, develop a bond between communities, and re-evaluate how we treat our planet.

If more people bought and ate locally produced food, it would reduce the demand for out of season, imported produce; therefore, the environmental footprint of importing goods could be reduced. It could also lessen the abuse by the country of origin, which might not have stringent laws and regulations for soil and water. They could be using many toxic sprays that cannot be washed off. There are sprays in use that are systemic, meaning the whole fruit will be contaminated and cannot be washed off. Monocultures of corn, soya, bananas, wheat and other produce are destroying much land everywhere. Oil palm plantations are especially catastrophic to rain forests, and products containing palm oil should be avoided.

The number one rule is: Read the label!

As well as making better fresh food choices, labels should always be scrutinized. Once the ingredients of a product are established, and we are sure it serves our health and beauty requirements, it should go onto our list of trusted products. Many tricks of the trade are used by industries to pull the wool over customer's eyes. I have established a rule for myself: don't buy what is heavily advertised. Good, nourishing, and basic foods seldom have a great deal of attention drawn to them. In my opinion, it is just as essential to read labels for all household products. This starts with personal items like soap, deodorant, face cream, shampoo, and such like. It should also continue with all household cleaning products, air fresheners, insect sprays, and of course flea and tick products for pets.

Unless labeled organic, degradable, and not tested on animals, all the personal items we find on the shelves on the supermarket contain chemicals of some sort - some are more toxic than others. Not only adults are exposed to them throughout their lives, but children and pets suffer just as much. I personally do my best to avoid products tested on animals. Would you have a product smeared into your dog's or cat's eyes to see if it does damage? Activists that free animals from laboratories are people I hold in high esteem. I must admit,

I could not do this myself. Seeing creatures suffer, just so we know it is safe to spray something on ourselves. I read a study revealing that women on average use 168 chemical compounds contained in their cosmetics, soap, shampoo, etc. per day, and men use about 85. Many of them are considered known carcinogens. Some of the common ingredients in lotions and potions are considered safe in small amounts but taken over a lifetime, it all adds up.

I personally know from patients in my clinic, and stories from friends and acquaintances, when they changed over to clean and organic products, allergies disappeared. When a friend finally stopped using hair dye, her skin rashes went away. The product she used was harmful and eventually compromised her immune system, hormone interruption etc. When the bucket is full...... To be fair, this does not mean there hadn't been other health problems present to cause allergies and similar symptoms. Nonetheless, it is a fact that many chemical compounds are the culprit in immune interruptions. There are certain artificial and toxic compounds we should know about and be aware of. Following is a list of the most used but beware there are many more.

- *Triclosan,* an anti-bacterial and anti-fungal agent which has been banned by the FDA in the USA from soaps and other body washes recently. It is still present in hand sanitizers and is also used in cleaners. I'm not sure if it is still in toothpaste and certain cosmetics.
- *Parabens* are preservatives used in most cosmetics, soaps, shampoos, skin care products and even baby products to extend shelf life.
- *Sodium Lauryl Sulfate, (SLS)* a lathering agent hidden in shampoo, soap, body wash and cleaning products, anything that froths up.
- *Mineral oil:* a petroleum byproduct found in some cosmetics, cheap skin products and even baby oil.
- *Propylene Glycol:* a hydrating agent keeping soaps, skin care products etc. moist.
- *Fragrances* - there are literally thousands of chemical fragrances made in laboratories. These are added to personal care products and air fresheners for homes. Perfumes consist mostly of artificially made fragrances, essential oils as a base would not last long.

- *Synthetic colours and dyes* are often added to make a product more attractive, but they are artificially made and should be avoided.
- *Formaldehyde* is a disinfectant and preservative.
- *Phthalates are* is a class of chemicals added as binding agents, and to make plastics flexible. Hardly any of them have been studied or tested. They are literally everywhere; most products contain one or more of them.

Then there is *Bisphenol A, BPA,* one of the most environmentally prevalent chemicals, mainly used in combination with other chemicals to manufacture plastics and resins. I am sure everyone has heard of the dangers of this chemical leaching from plastic bottles into the water or juice, especially when bottles are stored for a long time and/or stored in the sun or heat. It is also used in toys and in the lining of cans and probably in many other products. BPA can mimic human hormones and so disrupts the endocrine system. Lately it has been substituted by *Bisphenol S, BPS,* but apparently this isn't any better.

When we think back over a lifetime, or even just the last 10 years, how many of the chemicals, we have ingested? Plastic water bottles are everywhere and have been for years, but it is still a problem as they are used by so many regularly. The amount of crude oil used to make the plastics around the globe is immense and would be better used as fuel for cars etc. until we find another technology to drive our automobiles. There are many different plastics manufactured into a large range of bottles, tubs and take away containers. Industry likely find these too difficult or expensive to replace. It is best to avoid plastics where possible. It is possible to use very little plastic products, especially at home. Plastic wrap and bags can be substituted by products made of plant fibres; plastic bottles replaced with glass etc. We used to use glass, ceramic or metal containers to store food, why can't it be done today?

I am sure we have all seen photos of birds and marine animals that have been found dead, their stomachs full of discarded plastic. By ingesting the floating plastics, they starve to death. Many sea creatures are caught in or strangled by discarded plastic items; they die an awful death. *Microplastics* are tiny spheres, less than 5 millimetres in size, found all over the planet, originating from slowly disintegrating plastic material, which has been a concern for many years, and is found literally everywhere. They are now present in fresh water, seas and lakes, tap water and have even been found in bottled water.

I also have to mention *microbeads,* present in many personal care products like soap, shampoos, creams, age defying products, even toothpastes. Greenpeace calls them a toxic time bomb. Not everyone realizes they are made from all sorts of plastics. When using these products, the beads get swept into the drains, waterways and eventually into the ocean where they are ingested by marine life. They are so small; they cannot be removed. Some manufacturers have now stopped using them, so it is even more urgent to use organic, clean personal products not tested on animals. Research on personal care products and cosmetics by the Journal of Applied Microbiology in the UK shows many of those products, especially cosmetics, were found to be contaminated with different kinds of bacteria, amongst them E. Coli. Not only do we have microbeads and toxic ingredients in many products, we also have bacteria that is essentially harmful to us.

> *Please remember: Pets are exposed to all the micro-plastic and toxic ingredients just the same as we are and all wild animals as well.*

Manufacturing plastic items certainly won't end in a hurry, but what we *choose* to buy will tell manufacturers to clean up their act or go out of business. Hopefully, more new materials are researched and tested. Pineapple, aloe-vera, bamboo fibres and hemp have been in use for some years. A kind of leather made from plant fibres is already on the market. Many people think recycling is the solution to the plastic invasion. There aren't enough recycling plants to get a grip on the tonnes of plastic rubbish every day. Also, many articles are made from different kind of plastics, each needing a different method of recycling. Avoidance of any kind of artificial material is best.

Our choice in clothing can help some countries to prohibit children working in factories, and generally help people to receive a fair wage. Artificial, toxic dyes are used in cheap clothing, not only poisoning the people who manufacture them, but also contaminating rivers, lakes, and ground water. I often buy second-hand clothing, some of it is hardly or never worn and it is much cheaper than brand new. Second-hand shops are great to get pet blankets, baskets, and beds for a fraction of the price you pay in pet shops. Clothing, furniture, carpets, car seats, building materials, insulation material, electronics, just about everything in our homes is treated with flame retardant chemicals these days. It has even been found in infant mattresses and children's pyjamas! Washing hands frequently is suggested, but the chemicals leach from the fabrics, attach to the household dust, and so contaminate our homes. Pets have their noses closer to carpets and dust, being exposed to it even more than humans. They are also exposed when sleeping in newly bought beds and polyester filled mattresses, all a health risk. Even fire-fighters don't like flame retardants because of the toxic fumes released in a fire, creating a greater risk for their health, including cancer.

It is not up to any authority to tell us what to use, it is our responsibility to make choices at any minute, even no choice is a choice.

Self-help number 4: Become authentic

The definition of authentic in dictionaries is as follows: not false or copied, being genuine and real, representing one's own true nature and beliefs.

"Be yourself, everyone else is already taken."
Oscar Wilde

Our pets, really all animals, are teachers in that regard. The animals living amongst us or close by in the case of horses, even watching them in the wild, can help us to develop authenticity. As humans we want to fit in, be liked and accepted by others. As a result, the image we present is more like who we think we should be and often doesn't reflect who we really are. It certainly is not an easy task and can feel risky to present the real you. Just look at the Hollywood scene, celebrities pretending to be real people in the media. Magazines portray false images as trendy, put on nice faces, and tell people what they think they want to hear, because it's the 'done thing'. In my mind living authentically is much easier. One doesn't have to hide any feelings and thoughts, nor does anyone need to live a life to suit someone else's ideas of how things should be. Wearing a 'mask' at all times is hard and stressful and we can easily forget who we really are.

Being authentic basically means to come from within, when our words and actions are congruent with our values and beliefs. Authenticity does not know the word should. At times it certainly isn't easy to look at oneself and be happy what we see, nevertheless honesty is a good start to get to know oneself. As humans we certainly are complex beings, so taking time to look inward and getting to know our true self requires mindfulness and self-awareness. I suppose in our time and technological age it is far more difficult to find the true self. We are bombarded with so many messages, ideas and told what place we should occupy in society, so it is a constant balancing act to try to harmonize our inner and outer aspects. We are pushed to be even more perfect, more loveable, look better and at the same time hold a good job and own the appropriate gadgets to receive attention and be liked. As mentioned earlier in this book, growing up, we are moulded into a certain functional human by parents, teachers and peers, which results in learned ideas, thoughts, beliefs and behaviour. Rather than being our authentic self, we become an adaptive self. As I said earlier, I do not blame parents and teachers, they basically mean well. They want us to adapt to the ideas of the society we live in, because life is much easier that way and can be more rewarding, especially regarding being liked by others and of course the monetary reward is beckoning.

"The privilege of a lifetime is to become who you truly are."
Carl Jung

Many of us hear our inner voice pushing us to go past the fear and beyond the norm to find deeper meaning in our lives. Have the courage to acknowledge this voice, see it as a challenge to get to know yourself. Eventually, we recognize the feeling of being aware, which lets us see the discrepancies between our beliefs and actions. It also enables us to better identify the difference between saying things because that's what we were taught or simply saying what we really mean. It certainly is a learning process, and like everything else, it takes time to explore and examine doubts that might creep up. Getting rid of emotional baggage, growing and developing more self-esteem is a must on the road to authenticity.

We certainly have to know what we want and have the courage to follow through without worrying if the other people agree. We should be mindful of how our beliefs and actions influence or affect others. If we act with good intention and our motives are genuine, most people will admire our courage and integrity, and we could also be an example to them. A person acting authentically is also more open to new ideas and inspires others to feel free to be themselves. Putting time into personal growth, living, and embracing the moment is the best recipe.

I often watch dogs and cats doing their thing, oblivious to anything around them. I get the feeling they are totally immersed in what is at hand at that moment. They do one task at a time, there is no such thing as multi-tasking in the animal world. If they want something, they try to communicate it without trying to figure out if it is appropriate or not. If they want a cuddle, to have you play with them or to go for a walk, they just convey the message. They may do that with begging eyes, fetching their toys or leash, or just snuggling up with you on the couch. They don't think or fret at the thought of being turned down, they know there is a time later when the request is forthcoming, or they will simply 'ask' again. They are certainly aware of themselves, despite the failed mirror tests I have read about. Some scientists think if an animal can recognise themselves in a mirror and believe this shows they are aware of themselves as beings. In my opinion a vision test can't determine consciousness and awareness. This is really an area we do not have enough information about. It would help us to better understand them if we spent more time observing them. Not as a scientific mind, but as a human being open to learn from another species.

Take a leap into authenticity!

Self-help Number 5: Unconditional love - can we learn it?

When it comes to loving, our pets have no boundaries. Our appearance does not bother them, nor does that of any other animal for that matter. Bad haircut, not wearing the latest fashion, too skinny or a few kilos too heavy, they do not judge, they are always ready to accept us. They intuitively get a feel for our personality by reading our energy field as well as noticing our body language and facial expressions. This is how animals get to know each other. Humans want to be happy and joyful, which seems to be somehow difficult in our world today, being confronted with all the negativity and sadness. Unless we have good friends and/or family, it is more difficult to find much to laugh about. The world is filled with wars, environmental degradation, murders, cruelty and so much more on a daily basis. We also have a strong need to love and be loved, I believe it is the main reason we tend to gravitate to canine friends as they are honest, loving and genuine. They are comforting and great companionship for anyone, and great support for older and single people, children and adults challenged with physical or mental handicaps. Not to forget the spiritual uplifting they present us with when we suffer from trauma and depression, when we just can't understand the world anymore.

Pets love their humans unconditionally, whereas it is difficult for humans not to have any needs and expectations, or to be upset when things don't go our way. Is there such a thing as unconditional love in the human world? Unless we look at a mother's love for her children which is not bound by any conditions, it seems a difficult task for most people. We certainly wish for our relationships to be in a state of love and happiness, but it certainly does not mean to be a slave to anyone or fulfill a person's every need. Humans carry within them an inherent desire to remain in a state of love. When we stop looking outside ourselves for the level of love we desire and instead realize that we are a source of love ourselves, we shift our presence and inevitably everything shifts around us. When we look to ourselves for fulfillment, we attract circumstances that reflect similar states of being, our relationships with humans and/or pets become more fulfilling and easier.

It is hard to resist the gentle nudge of a wet nose or a lick on the hands from a dog and not feel the authentic love emanating from the animal. It certainly isn't just because the pet is hungry or wants to play, nothing really substitutes for their authenticity, they truly want to be with us. Stroking or petting a pet, no matter what animal it is, dog, rabbit, horse, lowers blood pressure and releases endorphins, it relaxes us and generally makes us feel wonderful.

Cats are more subtle in their ways, but nevertheless feel with and for us. They often come to us when we are down, pleased to see us or purr to make us feel comfortable. The frequency of their purring sound is between 25 and 140 Hz and interestingly it is the same frequency which aids in mending broken bones and general healing. Sound has been used for healing by many cultures for thousands of years, have cats 'invented' purring to heal themselves and for us to relax? Despite research, there are still many unanswered questions about cats purring. It does not necessarily mean they are happy and content, as it happens, they sometimes purr when in pain. Maybe to heal themselves? In any case, that sound generates such a feeling of wellbeing, as cat parents can vouch for. Having the cat close by or even better when she is sitting on our lap can make us feel happier. To me it is similar when chanting OM, the resonance within the body feels great. Their honesty, unconditional acceptance and love is of such a benefit for us, it can be a magical experience. It is this authentic and unconditional loving which draws us to pets. To have them in our lives lifts our mood and make us feel whole; the most important lesson for us all to learn. There is no need to bribe them with treats.

"A dog is the only thing on earth that loves you more than he loves himself."
Josh Billings

Self-help number 6: Caring for your pet

> *"Everyone thinks they have the best dog. And none of them are wrong."*
> *W.R. Purche*

Pets belong to the family and deserve what is best for their species - raw meat. It certainly starts with correct feeding, including some supplements not only for young and older animals, but for all. Considering our imperfect lifestyle and being inundated with unhealthy substances on a daily basis, which has been discussed thoroughly in previous chapters, there is still much we can do.

My feeding suggestions for dogs are simple: Discard all the hype and suggestions of the pet food industry, and feed fresh meat of different cuts. To save time and money, meat can be bought in bulk, frozen in portions and thawed out as needed. You might have a company in your area that delivers frozen meat or a friendly butcher who will prepare a monthly package for your dog. Minced off cuts from butchers also contain nutritious organ meat, rich in vitamins and minerals, sinews and cartilage. This is great as long as the animal gets bones or occasionally chunks of meat, lamb shanks or ox tails to keep teeth clean and exercise jaws. Don't worry about a bit of fat on the meat, animals need a certain amount like we do.

Cooking meat might be necessary for humans to destroy pathogens. Dogs get most nourishment from uncooked, raw meat. Proteins are not lost as quickly as vitamins when cooking meat, but certainly changes in the physical and chemical make-up occur. Water is lost (plus Vitamins), the collagen fibres shrink, and proteins become more resistant to digestive enzymes. Carnivores have evolved to eat raw meat for thousands of years. It is a fact that feeding raw meat protects them from bacterial contamination and food poisoning. It also reduces the chance of an obstruction when eating raw bones. If you change a dog or cat from a cooked, commercial diet to a raw one, introduce it slowly, taking at least 2 weeks. If done too quickly the animal might vomit or not eat it at all. It is best to start off with a small amount of fresh meat amongst what they usually eat and increase over time. Dogs are seldom a problem; cats can be fussy. It is a matter of persevering.

Chicken frames are also a good addition to your dog's diet, especially organic. Smaller breeds of dogs, and cats love chicken wings, but need to be introduced carefully when changing from commercial to raw foods. I personally would eat only organically grown chicken, the commercial ones are full of antibiotics, hormones and probably other chemicals and my dogs get the same. One or two eggs a week for dogs and egg yolks only for cats, is a great way to supply them with many Vitamins like some B Vitamins, Vitamin E, Zinc and Selenium. Eggs, especially the organic variety are very nourishing for us all.

The best time to feed dogs is in the morning or early afternoon, if possible. Similar to us, dogs should not eat late at night, especially the main meal right before they lie down for the night.

Dogs and cats should have bones daily if possible, especially when feeding pet mince which does not require much chewing. This can eventually cause plaque and bad breath. Gnawing on bones is great for canine and feline teeth, it keeps them clean, the meat and marrow is nourishing. The chewing motion activates saliva, gut bacteria, and enzymes to help digest and absorb nutrients. Moreover, it keeps them busy and happy, especially when left on their own. My dogs got a bone every morning when I left the house to go to work. None of them ever did silly things when alone, like chewing shoes and other items, digging holes or making noises to upset neighbours.

Dogs can have a little bit of vegetable in their feed, I recommend <u>finely</u> grated carrots and zucchini, and/or a <u>small</u> amount of cooked brown rice or cooked pumpkin peels. I do not recommend any other grains, potatoes, dairy or even leftovers from human dinners. Cats should **not** have any of the above, just different cuts of meat will do fine. Possibly adding some supplements if needed, like oils and probiotics, for older cats, maybe a joint supplement.

Even if pups are from healthy parents, I advise a mineral supplement. If their origins are not known or they are from a puppy mill, pet shop or the animal refuge, I would add probiotics and maybe an all-round vitamin formula. Many dogs are mineral deficient, due to the lack of nutrients in their parents feed, from growing up in a household feeding commercial pet foods, and possibly never having any bones to chew. The origins of deficiencies are not so dissimilar as with human babies and children and we see the results later in life in weak bones and joints, and other ailments. Adding natural enzymes in the form of sprouts is great. Especially *alfalfa* or *broccoli* sprouts, the latter is more expensive but full of good nutrients. Sprouts can be made from any grain or legume, providing it is organically grown. Share your home grown sprouts with your canine friend, a spoonful cut into their dinner helps to increase natural enzymes in the gut. Another idea is growing *wheat grass* and let the dogs or cats graze on it or, again, cut into their feed. A pot of *cat grass* is great for indoor cats who can't get to any fresh grass growing outside.

Coconut Oil, Flax Seed Oil or *Hemp Oil* are good additives for your dog (and for you), they help joints, make a shiny coat and are generally good for the body. There are many different supplements available for dogs and cats and, as mentioned earlier, it is a *must* to read the labels and avoid any supplements with chemical additives and fillers. Many are similar to human supplements, for instance *Glucosamine* and *Greenlip Mussels, Fish Oils, Sspirulina, Mushroom Complex* and others.

One supplement I personally recommend for humans and animals alike, is the powder from a tree called *Moringa Alternifolia*. This beautiful tree is native to Northern India. It is grown in warmer climate zones in some countries and known as a superfood in the western world. It has been used for hundreds, most probably thousands of years for its health giving and anti-inflammatory properties. Amazingly, the whole tree can be used: the bark and roots, the seeds made into a fine, hydrating oil, rich in vitamins used for the skin. The leaves are dried and sold as a supplement in powder form. Even the Egyptians and Romans used the oil, we know this from analysing the contents of amphoras buried in graves. Branches, leaves and flowers are found at Asian markets, eaten cooked or fried or drunk as a tea. *Moringa* has been used extensively in Indian Ayurvedic Medicine because of its high vitamin content, it has more iron than spinach and more Vitamin C than oranges. It is high in magnesium and is a protein source with 18 different amino acids and essential minerals. More information is available on many websites. Dogs and cats definitely benefit from added Moringa to their feed. Not only for increased health but also to detox many of the chemicals they ingest and take in via the skin.

Products I see as important, especially for dogs and cats having been fed a commercial diet, are *probiotics* and *digestive enzymes* designed to help the animals to regain their normal digestion and help to absorb the nutrients for a better overall bodily function. Even pet shops sell enzyme and probiotic formulas these days and there are websites with good products also. In times of stress probiotics also act as a preventative for tummy upsets.

Fulvic Acid, mentioned in an earlier chapter, is part of the decomposition of animal and plant matter over many thousands of years in nature, a product of microbial processes. It contains more than 70 trace elements and supplies humans and animals organisms with the compounds missing from soils these days. Taking *Fulvic Acid* can replace what vegetables and fruit are lacking as well as supplying our digestive system with good bacteria. There are supplements on the market specially designed for pets and farm animals.

Diatomaceous Earth, DE for short, is also a valuable addition to food for animals and humans alike. I could write a whole chapter about it; it is so versatile. It is like a clay, made from finely crushed freshwater organisms, high in silica, containing about 15 trace minerals and suitable for internal and external use. As we know silica is great for bones, cartilage, tendons and ligaments, skin, and hair, especially the amorphous form is easily absorbed and promotes digestion when taken on a daily basis. It is also used as a detox. It is fantastic as an internal supplement, and great for external use. Added to toothpaste or making your own using it as a base, as an exfoliant and beauty mask it will draw out impurities. There are many uses around the house, deodorizing shoes, cupboards, garbage bins, polishing metal, sprinkle around against cockroaches and other insects, also dusting leaves on plants kills insects. I use it on tomato plants against mould infections, works well.

All farm animals benefit from adding it to the feed and bedding to keep them free from pests. Sprinkled all over floors of chicken coops and providing a dust bath for them helps against mites. I suggest human grade DE for animals; for house and garden, use the industrial grade, which contains more crystalline silica. For dogs I recommend adding it to their feed, starting with a quarter or half a teaspoon for small dogs and obviously increasing this according to size. DE rubbed into a dog's coat, helps to keep fleas and ticks away. You can also dust their kennels and/or bedding with it. Cats also benefit from the powder, added to food for internal ingestion and externally if any skin problems occur.

We can often be overwhelmed looking at the shelves in pet shops and supermarkets - full of treats for cats and dogs. Here again, reading labels is crucial. Only buy treats made from various dried meat, liver and fish without additives. Personally, I have never given many treats, a dog chewing a bone a day or having one buried for later enjoyment, is quite happy without additional treats. Unhealthy treats, full of flour or other fillers contribute to weight problems, especially when given often.

A quick look at ear infections, as many dogs present with it. They can appear in various parts in the ears and are very often quite painful. Your dog will let you know by shaking, scratching or pawing at the ears, they could be smelly, have a waxy discharge or just be hot and inflamed. In severe cases a loss of balance or hearing loss will be noticed. Quite similar to the signs in people, especially children. Like any other conditions, there is usually an underlying problem. Antibiotics will stop the inflammation for a time but if the underlying cause is not addressed, the problem will recur. Apart from that, antibiotics will kill all bacteria, causing a bacterial imbalance and an overgrowth of yeasts is possible. Antibiotics are only a band aid, symptoms usually come back after some time. Remember that our world is full of chemicals not designed for living bodies. The diet that is fed to a dog has an impact on digestive health. The wrong diet is often the culprit, causing allergies which not only affects the ears, but also presents itself as an itchy or scaly skin, eczema, hair loss etc.

Dogs with long floppy ears can be prone to more ear infections, the long ears trap moisture, especially when swimming. They also have a greater area for things like grass seeds or ear mites to cause infections. Other reasons could also be wax build up. A healthy canine ear does not need cleaning and a little wax is normal. There are gentle, natural products available for cleaning ears and homeopathic remedies are also great to remove the cause. As said before, the diet needs to be changed to raw, possibly organic meats and supplements.

Essential oils can be useful for animals for physical and emotional situations, not only for humans. But keep in mind, their noses are hundred times more sensitive than ours, so caution is required, and the oils should be well diluted with carrier oils. Essential oils are 75 times stronger than the plant itself, this potency shouldn't be ignored. Be careful with strong smelling oils, like wintergreen, peppermint, cinnamon, clove, and eucalyptus, use them sparingly. Make sure the oils are from a reputable manufacturer and are high quality. Animal bodies are different from a human body so advice should be sought from a knowledgeable person if in doubt.

> *Because of their sensitive noses, diffusers and incense should not be used when animals are in the room!*

My suggestion for a rinse for dogs is as follows: about 5 drops each of rosemary, tea tree and lavender, occasionally adding a small amount of peppermint, in half a bucket of water. This helps to keep fleas, mosquitos, and other mites away. To get the rinse water amongst the fur in long haired dogs, a few drops of organic shampoo or soap can be added, but only minimal. Personally, I do not think bathing dogs too often is good for them. The oils naturally occurring on the skin, are important for skin health and bathing them too often interferes with this. So, we now look at shampoos we can safely use for dogs. Remember, any skin conditions have an internal cause and cannot be fixed with fancy or medical shampoos. I use a mild, organic shampoo, not tested on animals for myself and suggest the same for dogs. There are now hair soap bars available in health food shops which would be an alternative. Any harsh soaps or shampoos will irritate the skin and remove the naturally occurring oils.

Fleas and other parasites mostly attach to weaker animals, this is easily spotted when there are several animals in a household. It pays out to have healthy, robust pets, and use some simple home remedies. They should always be nontoxic to the animal and humans. Flea collars are a great concern! Rinses and spot liquids are a chemical cocktail of neuro toxins, affecting the whole of the animal. Those products are designed to go in the bloodstream and so poison the fleas, unfortunately, they also poison the dog. In nature, evolution has not designed a dog's organisms to deal with deadly toxins. These burden their liver and affect the nervous system. In mild cases skin irritations appear, but can cause tremors, epileptic fits and even death!

There is a similar problem with heartworm tablets; these medications are also attacking the nervous system of the animals in the long term. They only kill the larvae of the heartworm not the adult parasite. Many holistic vets do not recommend any heartworm medication but suggest blood testing if not sure. When we think of a strong immune system, we automatically think of preventing illness like kennel cough or parvo, but the immune system also wards off parasites. So, any healthy, <u>thriving</u> animal will have minimal parasites. Since the heartworm is transferred by mosquitos, the best prevention is to protect from bites. You can use the daily flea and mosquito rinses I recommended earlier if you live in an area where mosquitos are common. It does not make sense to poison the dog just to get rid of parasites.

Vaccinations are also weakening the animal. I do not understand giving an animal, or a human for that matter, toxic substances that possibly cause cancer, neurological issues, and/or viral infections because of a lowered immune system. Healthy and strong organisms are designed by nature to seek out viruses and pathogens and remove them. Personally, I do not believe in vaccinations or any unnatural treatments; supporting the natural defence mechanism in animals (as well as in humans of course) is the way to overcome many health challenges. Everyone has to decide this for themselves, there is much information and reading material on offer. Concerned holistic vets are voicing their opinions on the matter. In serious and life-threatening situations, we certainly call professional help.

Prevention, as always, is the best medicine!

It certainly makes a difference if the pups, kittens, foals or other animals are born from healthy strong parents in a caring environment or have been subjected to stresses, either in the womb, by the birth process or growing up. Any of which could influence their health and behaviour in later life. This is known as primary reflexes, often not recognised as such and animals are chastised for bad or unwanted behaviour we cannot explain. Looking into the heritage and upbringing of an animal is paramount to understanding the cause of its behaviour. Rescued animals often show such problems and need a gentle helping hand to trust again and enjoy life. A toxic overload, mental, physical or emotional can significantly reduce the quality of life and keep us from enjoying the time with our pets. So, how do we create balance and harmony within our body? We start with healing the gut and eliminating the toxins within our body and that of our pets. The most effective way to do that is with a detox. I touched on Diatomaceous Earth earlier but repeat D.E. is very efficient to bind toxins so they can be released and taken out of the body.

It is common sense that a dirty house needs cleaning.

Being conscious of our voice when talking to any animal is something to learn, especially finding the right tone with our own pets. The voice we use in instructing the pets is of consequence to effectively communicate with them. A low, decisive and confident voice repeating the same commands are appreciated by dogs trying to please us. They are smart and sensitive to hear the undertones and aren't fooled easily. When dealing with animals, we have a chance to learn honesty, listening to our own words. Do we mean what we say? Do we say what we mean? Educating dogs is easy, especially when we are fortunate to have them from puppyhood onwards. We are the parent, carers and protectors to them. They will copy us and follow our cues and instructions. The situation is different when an older animal joins us, especially abused dogs might have problems fitting in. It takes a great deal of patience; trust has to be established first and then a bit of psychology applied. Cats are different as everyone knows, but nevertheless they deserve the same TLC as any other animal. They are just as loving, but don't show it exuberantly like dogs do.

Going for walks, play and time together need to be part of a daily routine. Dogs get bored like we do and might get up to silly things if not able to romp and play. Not only is playing great for coordination, muscle building and mental stimulation, but it is also a big part of socializing with their canine friends - who knows, they might exchange news about their humans. Dogs of all sizes, breeds and age enjoy freedom to express themselves in play, it benefits their overall health and wellbeing. Games are a fantastic way of bonding with your pup and playfully educating him or her at the same time and getting rid of the surplus energy, so you can both enjoy a quiet night.

Different breeds have different needs. It is important to think about the time we have available each day for play and exercise before we acquire a pet. There is much information to be found in books, internet or from reputable breeders. People often assume that small breeds do not need much exercise which isn't quite the case. Knowing what 'purpose' a breed was originally bred for is important to know. This helps you to give the animal the space and physical activity it needs. A Cattle dog or Kelpie needs to run and prefers to 'work' in comparison to a Labrador or Setter. Working dogs should not be in small yards unless they are older and are pensioners. It is a matter of common sense and in the interest of the animal's wellbeing.

Cats are easier, not requiring their people to go for walks, although there are people who take cat for walks on a harness. Some adjust to it easily; others do not like it at all. If they have enough space to play, like in a back yard, a tree stump or scratch post to keep their claws exercised and of course places around the house to curl up on, they are happy and content. Obesity in pets has increased in the last twenty years so daily exercise, walks, fetching balls or swimming is great to steadily lose weight. Of course, food and supplements should be adjusted accordingly, so it is easier for the animal to shed the weight. As a pet ages, even just a few pounds will have an effect on heart health and put more pressure on joints.

What is more enjoyable than going for a walk in nature, a forest, open meadow or even a leafy suburb with a furry four-legged friend. If you are lucky to have a beach nearby, even better. Sea air, swimming and walking in the sand are invigorating and fun for all. Dog parks are another great place to meet, not just for dogs, also for their humans enjoy meeting other canine lovers for a chat, sharing a common interest and enjoyment. I am pleased to say that a greater number of people walking their dogs on harnesses instead of leads on collars. It takes the pressure off the neck and distributes it around the back. For me there is another reason, I do not lead a friend from around the neck. Fancy and practical harnesses, for puppies, dogs that pull and just for safety are offered in all pet shops and on many websites. A harness should be made of strong material, particularly for larger breeds, and fit well. They should be softer with more padding for a sensitive animal and the small breeds. Some designs are called vests. When well made, they are extremely safe and secure. Of course, they need to be adjustable for the best fit. If the dog is not friendly with strangers or you want to keep children from approaching, you can have a warning stitched on the harness or vest, it saves telling people every time.

We not only walk our dogs for fun and exercise. It gives them a chance to 'read the newspaper' as I call it, namely smelling where other canines have been and left their mark. It is in the interest of the dog to let them stop and start and give them time to smell whatever is important for them. I bet their sensitive noses can tell who has been before, what mood they were in, or what they had for dinner. I often see people pulling their animal away from those delicious smells, not fair I feel. It is important for them to pee on other dog's deposits and they need to find the right spot to do their business, that is their custom. Most dog parents have poo bags floating around in handbags, pockets, or cars, just in case, I know I have. But we should make sure to source recyclable ones these days with all the plastics polluting the landfills. At least we can question pet shop owners and make sure our needs are known. If no one asks nothing will be done.

De-clutter your mind and meditate with your animal. Sit quietly, close to your pet, open your heart and mind, and just let it flow. Align your breath with that of your dog. It might not happen straight away but persevere without forcing yourself. Animals have a much quieter mind than ours, so we can learn and take our cues from them - get to know ourselves, release stress, deepen our connection and positively merge with another species. This could help us humans to overcome grief, depression, anxiety, fear or loneliness and might open the door to unconditional love. Even being amongst a herd of cows, riding on your horse or being amongst any other animal group out in the wild can be a meditation, creating awareness and mindfulness about one's life. What a great feeling, having quiet moments with a purring cat on your lap, pure meditation!

Playtime - Happy Days!

Self-help number 7: Have fun, fun, fun.

> *"We don't stop playing because we grow old,*
> *we grow old because we stop playing."*
> *George Bernhard Shaw*

Never mind what age, fun can be had by everyone. Again, play and fun relieves stress, improves relationships and connections, keeps the mind sharp and is anti-aging to top it off. How can we refuse to have fun and enjoyment? A guarantee to brighten your life is having a puppy or kitten, they are just hilarious to watch and play with. Pets and children are the best examples of how simple and entertaining fun can be. As adults, we still have a need to play, not work or be serious all the time. We are Beings - not Doings. The added bonus of play and having fun is laughter, the brain releasing endorphins, the feel-good hormone keeping us on an even keel and feeling well, counteracting any bad moods. What are we waiting for?

> *Enjoy time with your pet to the fullest, see the beauty of life -*
> *good vibrations will spread everywhere!*

About the Author

From an early age, Regine has felt a strong connection to nature and the passion never wavered throughout her life. Her training as a Naturopath and other associated therapies, like Iridology, Homeopathy, Hypnotherapy, gave her more understanding how we, as humans, are intertwined with all creatures great and small.

Regine also taught Meditation and Qi Gong classes which she learned on her travels to China. For more than thirty years, she helped many people with Laser Acupuncture and occasionally treated a dog for joint problems as well. Growing herbs and how to use them in cooking and for beauty treatments has always been a pet subject of Regine's. Apart from working in her clinic, she raised a variety of animals on her farms as well as training horses and going on horse treks in Far North Queensland.

Regine's main interests are to empower her clients to live a healthier and a less stressful life and to share her knowledge and practical experience with everyone, so we all contribute to making this planet a better place. For the last three years, Regine has been studying and travelling with the Resonance Science Foundation, learning about Quantum Physics which describes nature at the smallest scale of energy levels of atoms and subatomic particles. This is the basis of life and brings everything together.

White Light
PUBLISHING

www.ingramcontent.com/pod-product-compliance
Lightning Source LLC
Chambersburg PA
CBHW051538010526
44107CB00064B/2769